The
DARK GAME

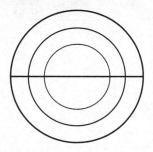

GAME

TRUE SPY STORIES FROM
INVISIBLE INK TO CIA MOLES

Paul B. Janeczko

CANDLEWICK PRESS

First paperback edition 2012

The Library of Congress has cataloged the hardcover edition as follows:

Janeczko, Paul B.
The dark game : true spy stories / Paul B. Janeczko. —1st ed.
p. cm.
ISBN 978-0-7636-2915-1 (hardcover)
1. Espionage, American—History—Anecdotes—Juvenile literature.
2. Espionage—United States—History—Anecdotes—Juvenile literature.
3. Spies—United States—Biography—Anecdotes—Juvenile literature.
4. Military intelligence—United States—History—Anecdotes—Juvenile literature.
5. United States—History, Military—Anecdotes—Juvenile literature.   I. Title.
UB271.U5J36 2010
327.73—dc22   2009049102

ISBN 978-0-7636-6066-6 (paperback)

13 14 15 16 17 BVG 10 9 8 7 6 5 4 3

Printed in Berryville, VA, U.S.A.

This book was typeset in Melior Medium.

Candlewick Press
99 Dover Street
Somerville, Massachusetts 02144

visit us at www.candlewick.com

For John and Lori Gunn:
good neighbors don't need fences

CONTENTS

INTRODUCTION

Whenever I visit schools to talk to students about my writing and my books, someone always asks this question: "Did you always want to be a writer?" Far from it. Being a writer was probably the furthest thing from my mind when I thought of what I wanted to be when I grew up. More than anything else, I wanted to be an FBI agent. Seriously.

Looking back, it's easy for me to understand why I found such a career so appealing. Nearly all that I read, outside of the usual stuff for school, was about crime and detection. I was a huge fan of the Hardy Boys. *That* was the life I wanted to lead, even though my father fixed televisions for his work and my brothers and I were more interested in playing baseball.

Beyond the Hardy Boys books, I read whatever I could find on crime and detection in our town library or in the used bookshop that I regularly visited. I read about gangsters, like Al Capone and Legs Diamond, and about the federal agents who fought them, like Eliot Ness and the Untouchables. I read books like *The FBI in Peace and War, Inside the FBI,* and *The FBI Story* and marveled at the way they tracked down criminals and spies. But I didn't stop with books on the FBI. I read books about the U.S. Secret Service and U.S. treasury agents to find out how they helped protect our country from saboteurs. If it was about espionage, I probably read it.

My fascination with spies didn't stop with my reading as a kid. As I grew up, I continued to feed my fascination with the espionage game and those who practiced it by reading novels by writers like Eric Ambler, John Buchan, and John LeCarré. Later I read spy tales by Robert Ludlum and Alan Furst. But I also followed the real-life spy dramas that were unfolding in the news, like ill-fated U.S. spy flights of the U-2 and the bugging of the American embassy in Moscow, both of which I include in this book.

But I never knew anything about the history of spies in this country. I didn't know that George Washington was instrumental in establishing an intelligence community in the colonies that played a huge role in winning the Revolutionary War. I knew nothing about the women who acted as spies during the Civil War. Nor did I know that the espionage establishment grew and changed as our country went to war, that it adapted to new technologies. And although I'd read a lot about espionage since the start of World War II, I knew only part of the story. The research I did to write this book filled in the gaps.

Spying is a murky business: it's not always easy to tell the good guys from the bad guys, you're not always certain who is telling the truth, and those you call your friends might not be who you think they are. Indeed, the spy's world can be a deadly place. Nonetheless, men and women continue to work in the shadows, trying to serve the government and citizens of their country.

The other side of the spy story is the work of the counterintelligence agents who track down spies in a frantic effort to stop the damage they have done. In chapter 6 you can read about the CIA and FBI agents who gathered evidence against Aldrich Ames and Robert Hanssen. These agents also work in the center of the spy game.

Since you have picked up this book, I'm guessing that your interest in spies may run as deeply as mine. I wrote this book because I wanted to make available to young readers something of a history of spying as it affected the United States from the Revolutionary War through the Cold War and into the end of the twentieth century. The story continues, of course, with the terrorist attacks of 9/11 and beyond. But that is a subject for another book. In the meantime, I hope you enjoy this one.

Outspying the British

I f ever there was a war that showed the importance of intelligence gathering, it was the American Revolution. When the colonies went to war to free themselves from the grip of King George III, they had no centralized government. Thus, they had no federal army, only local militias, and no central treasury with which to outfit and arm those militias. And, of course, they had no organized intelligence network. Despite all these shortcomings, the colonists defeated the mighty British Empire. How did that happen? Historians generally agree with British major George Beckwith, the head of British intelligence operations in America at the end of the war, who wrote, "Washington did not really outfight the British, he simply outspied us!"

The colonies' spy network developed slowly. First came organized resistance to British actions, in the form of secret societies called the Sons of Liberty—the first of which was formed in Boston in 1765. Branches of the Sons of Liberty were created in all the New England colonies, then in New York and South Carolina.

As the political climate heated up, Samuel Adams wanted to get the word out across the colonies and so formed the first Committee of Correspondence in Boston in 1772. Soon, more than eighty communities in the Massachusetts colony had similar committees, and the idea spread down the East Coast. The Committees' main purpose was to alert colonists to the latest actions of the British. They also organized express riders to deliver Patriot propaganda—material that could not be sent via the Crown's official post offices—to rally colonists to the cause.

The work of the Committees of Correspondence developed into the Committees of Safety around 1775. These committees carried the Patriot agenda a step closer to war. Their mission was military, including activating militia and confiscating British or Tory weapons and stores.

Around the same time, in Samuel Adams's hometown of Boston—often called the Cradle of Liberty—some local Patriots formed what many historians consider the first intelligence-gathering network in the colonies. The group was known as the mechanics because its members, including Paul Revere, were skilled laborers and artisans. The mechanics snooped on British activities and also sabotaged and stole British military equipment.

George Washington and the Culper Spy Ring

Seven months after the war started on the common of Lexington, Massachusetts, the Second Continental Congress intensified its efforts to gather and manage intelligence. The group's most significant decision came when it named George Washington as the director of the fledgling intelligence operation. So the man who would become the "father of our country" can also be considered the father of American espionage. For the remainder of the war, George Washington served the dual role of commander in chief of the rebel troops and director of espionage operations.

During the early months of the war, things did not go well for the rebels. On August 20, 1776, 20,000 British troops under General William Howe arrived on Long Island to confront Washington's troops. A week later, the rebels retreated and, under the cover of a thick night fog, evacuated by boat to Manhattan. Although Washington avoided almost certain capture, Howe was not willing to let him off the hook so easily. His redcoats landed at Manhattan's Kip's Point in September and pursued the rebel army until it was driven up Manhattan Island to Harlem Heights.

With the British army controlling New York City, Washington knew the city would be teeming with redcoats, affording him no better place to gather military intelligence. He set out to establish a spy network in the city. He asked Major Benjamin Tallmadge of the 2nd Continental Light Dragoons to reorganize and improve the spy network in the New York City area. Using the code name of John Bolton, Tallmadge established a spy network that enjoyed tremendous success for the duration of the war.

Washington instructed Tallmadge that each spy should gather as much useful intelligence as he could. Washington suggested that Tallmadge's agents blend in with the local population, especially members of the British Army. Of course every spy was to pay particular attention to troop movements by land and sea. In addition, Washington wanted the spies to find out how many soldiers were in the city and where they were stationed. Also they were to report on the food, supplies, and fuel, and the "Health and Spirits of the Army, Navy, and City." In other words, spies were charged with noticing everything that might assist the Continental army. A tall order!

The main player in Tallmadge's New York City spy ring was Abraham Woodhull of Setauket, Long Island. Under the code name of Samuel Culper, later changed to Samuel Culper Sr., Woodhull moved to New York City and began spying for the Patriots. A slight man who rarely spoke above a whisper, Woodhull visited markets and coffeehouses, keeping his eyes and ears open for any useful information.

Woodhull lived in constant fear of being discovered. Of course, living in the same boardinghouse as British soldiers did nothing to put him at ease. On one spring night in 1779 as Woodhull sat hunched over his desk, writing a secret message in invisible ink, the door to his room flew open. In horror, the spy sprang from his chair and upset his desk, spilling the valuable ink. The intruders? Not, as he had feared, British soldiers sent to arrest him, but two women friends who wanted to surprise him!

Woodhull's fear of discovery grew. "I live in daily fear of death and destruction," he wrote. "This added to my usual anxiety hath almost unmanned me." In addition, he learned that his absence from his Long Island home was beginning to arouse suspicions. Apparently, someone had reported his prolonged absence to the British, and a detachment of Queen's Rangers had ransacked his house. Woodhull decided to "work from home," back on Long Island, but not before he found someone to take his place in the city.

By the end of the month, Woodhull wrote Tallmadge to say that he had found his replacement: "a faithful friend and one of the first characters in the city to make it his business and keep his eyes upon every movement and assist me in all respects." Woodhull was speaking of his friend Robert Townsend, the man who was to become Samuel Culper Jr.

Good-looking and charming, Townsend had a number of advantages over Woodhull. For one thing, as a dry-goods merchant, he was able to make frequent deliveries from Manhattan to Long Island without raising suspicions of any observant Loyalist. His business also allowed him to write frequent letters, which provided excellent cover for sending and receiving invisible ink messages. In addition, Townsend's father lived on Long Island—conveniently, about a dozen miles from Woodhull's house in Setauket. Finally, the young spy had a flair for journalism and wrote occasional stories for the *Royal Gazette,* a favorite Tory newspaper. And as a journalist, he could mingle freely with the redcoats who visited New York City's bars, theaters, and coffeehouses. Always happy to see a few kind words about themselves in the *Gazette,* British soldiers spoke freely to Culper Jr., unaware that they were aiding the enemy.

With Townsend's excellent cover and contacts, it wasn't long before valuable military intelligence—including information about troop strength, deployment, and morale—was on its way to General Washington. When it was time to convey intelligence, Townsend used a courier—usually his customer Austin Roe—to carry the written reports to Culper Sr. on Long Island.

Townsend rarely met Woodhull personally—that would be too risky. Like a lot of spies since then, the Culpers used what's known as a dead drop. Here's how theirs worked: When Roe arrived in Setauket, he went to Woodhull's rear pasture, which Roe had rented for his cattle. At the pasture, Roe made a show of checking his cattle (to satisfy any curious neighbors) before slipping away to a far corner where a small box was buried. Roe placed his intelligence in the box and then returned to New York.

Abraham Woodhull meets Caleb Brewster, a boatman for the Culper spy ring, who frequently crossed Long Island Sound with intelligence.

I		J		M		Q/O	
s	280	purge	336	mort	382	ow	433
if	281	July	337	mind	383	or	434
in	282	jury	338	many	384	out	435
is	283	jealous	339	mercy	385	offer	436
it	284	justify	340	moment	386	office	437
ice	285	January	341	murder	387	onset	438
ink	286			measure	388	order	439
into	287	**K**		method	389	over	440
instance	288	key	342	mischief	390	obstruct	441
island	289	king	343	mistake	391	obtain	442
impress	290	kill	344	molest	392	observe	443
improve	291	know	345	majesty	393	occur	444
incamp	292			meditate	394	offence	445
incur	293	**L**		memory	395	omit	446
insert	294			messenger	396	oppose	447
inforce	295			misery	397	obligate	448
instance	296	laws	346	moveable	398	obstinate	449
insnare	297	land	347	multitude	399	obviate	450
intricel	298	love	348	miscarry	400	occupy	451
intrigue	299	low	349	misfortune	401	operate	452
intrust	300	lot	350	miserable	402	origin	453
instant	301	lord	351	mercenary	403	ornament	454
invert	302	light	352	majority	404	overcome	455
invite	303	fact	353	minority	405	overlook	456
ignorant	304	learn	354	memorial	406	overtake	457
imprudent	305	lady	355	mysterious	407	overrun	458
industry	306	letter	356	manufacture	408	overthrow	459
infamous	307	levy	357	moderator	409	obedience	460
influence	308	love-new	358	ministerial	410	objection	461
infantry	309	liar	359	**N**		october	462
infantry	310	lucky	360	name	411	obscure	463
injury	311	language	361	news	412	occasion	464
innocent	312	limit	362	no	413	opinion	465
instrument	313	liquid	363	not	414	oppression	466
intimate	314	longitude	364	night	415	opportunity	467
allege	315	latitude	365	never	416	obligation	468
imagin	316	laudable	366	needful	417		
important	317	legible	367	number	418	**P**	
imprison	318	liberty	368	neither	419	pay	469
interest	319	lottery	369	nothing	420	peace	470
incumber	320	literature	370	neglect	421	plan	471
inhuman	321			nation	422	put	472
enquiry	322	**M**		navy	423	port	473
interview	323	man	371	natural	424	proof	474
incorrect	324	map	372	negative	425	please	475
interceed	325	may	373	negligence	426	part	476
interfere	326	march	374	november	427	paper	477
intermix	327	marl	375	necessary	428	pardon	478
introduce	328	make	376	nobility	429	party	479
immediate	329	met	377	**O**		perfect	480
impatient	330	me	378	oath	430		
encourage	331	my	379	of	431		
insurrection	332	much	380	off	432		
irregular	333	move	381				
overload	334						
indians	335						

30742

A page from Major Tallmadge's codebook. Note the columns of words and their corresponding secret numbers.

Culper Sr. later took a leisurely stroll through his pastures to retrieve the information that Roe had left in the box. Safely back in his house, he looked out his window across Conscience Bay to the home of Anna Strong, who used laundry on her clothesline to signal Culper Sr. If Culper Sr. saw a black petticoat hanging from the line, he knew that Caleb Brewster, a rough and adventuresome Patriot, had arrived in his whaleboat and was waiting to carry any intelligence across the Devil's Belt (now known as Long Island Sound) to Tallmadge in Connecticut. Woodhull would then count how many handkerchiefs were hanging on the line to determine which of six hidden coves Brewster was waiting in.

At first, the Culpers sent their intelligence in a code concocted by Major Tallmadge. It was a simple code, but it served them well throughout the war. Tallmadge combed through *Entick's Dictionary* until he came up with a list of about seven hundred words most likely to be needed in a Culper secret message. Then he assigned each word a number. For example, *advise* was 15, *knowledge* was 345, *time* was 633, and *troops* was 645. In addition to these common words, names of important people and places were also part of Tallmadge's codebook.

One of the letters that Culper Sr. sent shows how the code numbers were used:

Every 356 [letter] is opened at the entrance of 727
[New York City], and every one is searched. They
have some 345 [knowledge] of the route that our
356 [letters] take. . . . I intend to visit 727 [New York
City] before long and think by the assistance of a
355 [lady] of my acquaintance, shall be able to out-
wit them all.

This excerpt raises one of the most tantalizing mysteries of the American Revolution. You'll notice in the last sentence that Culper mentions 355, the code number for *lady*. This number appears frequently in the Culpers' letters and seems to refer to a specific woman who was an active member of their spy ring. But the facts about this mystery woman are scant. We know that she lived in New York. That Woodhull thought that she could "outwit them all" has led historians to believe that she was already involved in espionage before Robert Townsend met her. Historians also believe that she and Townsend had a son and that she was ultimately arrested by the British for her activities. There are no further clues about her identity in any correspondence or diary entries.

In *A Peculiar Service,* author Corey Ford speculates about 355. He asks, "Did her social position enable her to gain access to highly classified British intelligence, some of it known only to the Commander-in-Chief and his aide?" In other words, was British Major John André—who was involved with Benedict Arnold and later hanged as a spy—captivated by 355's charms and flirtations? After all, André did have a reputation for surrounding himself with women of intelligence and beauty.

Ford hypothesizes that when Major André left with General Henry Clinton for North Carolina, 355 and Robert Townsend spent more time together and fell in love. But marriage would have been out of the question if they were both to continue their undercover work. Ford surmises that this conflict could account for Townsend's abrupt announcement in April 1780 that he was leaving the Culper ring. Without Townsend's leadership, the ring shut down.

Not for long, though: Robert Townsend's "retirement" lasted only about sixty days. He returned to his spy work as abruptly as he had left it and gave no explanation for his return. It could be that he felt guilt and remorse for abandoning his patriotic duty. It could likewise be that he and 355 had separated over their conflict and he hoped that working with the Culper ring would give him the chance to see her again. However, any joy he might have felt reuniting with his love did not last long.

In late October, 355 was arrested, along with Hercules Mulligan, another member of the Culper ring, on the charge of spying—the only members of the spy ring to ever be so accused. Mulligan ran a tailor shop frequented by British officers and regularly passed along to Washington bits of intelligence that he overheard in his shop. The genial Irish immigrant was able to talk his way out of the arrest, but not 355. The evidence against her was too strong. Benedict Arnold, newly arrived in the city, was convinced that she was involved in the uncovering of his plan to surrender West Point to the British. Accordingly, 355 was convicted of spying and condemned without a trial.

Her arrest was shocking enough for Townsend, but he was crushed when he learned that the redcoats had locked up a "woman spy" on the HMS *Jersey,* the oldest of five waterlogged and squalid prison ships anchored in Wallabout Bay, on the Brooklyn side of the East River. The ship was nicknamed *Hell,* and the guards saw to it that the name was apt. Some sources report that nearly 12,000 prisoners perished on the jail ships.

Ford imagines Robert Townsend, heartbroken, taking a nighttime walk to the end of Murray's Wharf and staring into the darkness that concealed the *Jersey.* He could not visit 355, the woman who was carrying his child. He couldn't even let it be known that he knew her, for fear of endangering the lives of the other members of the Culper operation. In Ford's imagined scene, Townsend gives a final look in the direction of the prison ship, then walks back to his boardinghouse room, packs his bag, and leaves New York.

Townsend was eventually able to rescue his son from the prison ship and lived with his sister in the country until he died at the age of eighty-four. And 355? Her bones were buried in a common grave for the prison ship victims. As Ford wrote, "355 remains as anonymous in death as she was in life, an American heroine without a name."

The skill of the Culpers led to an impressive list of achievements. For example, late in 1779, they uncovered a plot by British agents to smuggle counterfeit money into Connecticut to help the Loyalists pay their taxes and devalue Continental currency. It was probably Townsend who picked up this bit of intelligence as he carefully eavesdropped on conversations among British officers in a Manhattan coffee shop. The Culpers remained a constant, reliable source of military intelligence for most of the war. We can only guess how the war might have gone differently without their daring secret service.

Benjamin Franklin

IN 1775, THE SECOND CONTINENTAL CONGRESS created the Committee of Secret Correspondence to gather intelligence, establish communication with Patriot sympathizers in Great Britain and elsewhere, and also seek alliances with foreign nations. It chose sixty-nine-year-old Benjamin Franklin to lead the European delegation.

In October 1776, Franklin sailed to Paris along with Silas Deane and Dr. Arthur Lee; their goal was to induce the French monarchy to support the colonies in their fight against England. Seeking aid from France was a logical step since France and England had been bitter rivals for years. In addition, France had her eyes on the high dividends that trade with the colonies could pay. For the Americans, the appeal to France was made in desperation. As Robert Morris, a member of Congress, wrote to Franklin, "In a Word, Sir, we must have it."

In addition to securing much needed assistance from France, Franklin and his associates became deeply involved in espionage activities. One of their specialties was creating and distributing propaganda. One of Franklin's most creative acts of propaganda was a letter purportedly written by a Prussian prince to the commander of the Hessian mercenaries who were fighting for the British. In the letter, the "prince" complained

Benjamin Franklin: inventor, elder statesman, and propagandist for the colonies

over the low casualty figures among Hessian troops. The British were paying him a bounty, he said, for each Hessian killed in battle, so, in order to keep casualty numbers up, he recommended that any wounded Hessians be left for dead. After all, "a crippled man," as he put it, is of no use as a soldier.

This masterpiece of propaganda was widely circulated in Europe, as well as in the colonies among the Hessians. The reaction from Europe sharply criticized the royal government for paying "blood money" for foreigners whose governments "sold" their citizens to the British. Franklin didn't stop there. With his connections back in the colonies, he was able to fashion a fake Boston newspaper. Among local legitimate news and ads, Franklin added an article or two of his own. One article explained how the British were paying their Indian allies a bounty for each scalp they could turn in. The "reporter" noted that many of the scalps looked to be taken from women and children. Needless to say, this bit of misinformation caused a firestorm in England and gave the Whig critics of the war "facts" to bolster their opposition.

Benjamin Franklin also used his skill at deception on the French. After the rebels had won a decisive victory over the British at Saratoga, New York, in the fall of 1777, the British began making peace overtures to the colonies. The French, though impressed with the victory of the rebels over a larger army, were still hesitant to commit themselves to a formal military alliance with the Americans. To nudge the French further along the road to an alliance, Franklin agreed to speak with the British about a possible reconciliation. Even though he had no intention of making peace with the British, he knew that if there was one thing that the French did not want, it was an American reconciliation with England. Franklin's "perception management" (or out-and-out deception, some might say) did the trick. He knew that word would get back to the French about his meeting with the British. So it was that on February 6, 1778, the French Royal Council signed a treaty to enter into an offensive and defensive alliance that would prove to be a lifeline for the colonies in their battle against England.

The significance of Franklin's work for the rebel cause in France cannot be minimized. The French provided 90 percent of the gunpowder used by the rebels in the first years of the war. In addition, France pumped tens of millions of dollars into the war effort and supplied troops, officers, and naval support. In fact, when General Cornwallis surrendered to the Continental army at Yorktown, Virginia, in 1781, ending the war, there were more French troops than American troops present.

Benedict Arnold

While Benedict Arnold is remembered by most people as a spy and a traitor, few know that he served as a daring and courageous officer in the Continental army. In fact, some historians believe that the war would have been lost without his early battlefield heroics. Nonetheless, this fearless officer went on to betray the country he served for many years.

Arnold was born in 1741 in Norwich, Connecticut, and, at fourteen years old, he ran away from home to fight in the French and Indian War (1755–1763). Whether he actually fought in the war is open to debate. Regardless, Arnold had gotten a taste for life in the military and joined the Continental army in the spring of 1775. So began a military career in which Arnold distinguished himself on the battlefield time and again. Washington would come to consider Arnold to be his finest field commander.

Arnold lost no time making a name for himself in the army. He hurried to Boston at the start of the Revolutionary War to work with Patriot leaders. He led a victorious attack on Fort Ticonderoga and secured twenty-one cannons that the rebels dearly needed. He was rewarded by being named colonel of a company of Massachusetts soldiers.

Arnold's reputation as a brave warrior continued to grow when his men joined the forces of General Richard

Montgomery and attacked the British stronghold on Quebec. The fighting was fierce, resulting in a serious leg wound for Arnold, who spent the next six months recuperating. Once his leg healed, he accepted his next assignment as commander of a seventeen-ship fleet on Lake Champlain, on the border between New York State and Vermont.

Although Arnold had reason to believe that his heroism and valor would be rewarded, he was sorely disappointed. The Continental Congress passed him over for promotion, instead promoting five officers with less experience. To add to this insult, the Massachusetts colony authorities refused to reimburse him for military expenses that he had paid out of his own pocket. The final blow came when he received news that his wife had died while he was away from his Connecticut home. Angry and dispirited, Benedict Arnold went home to New Haven.

In late April of 1777, however, he got word that the British were retreating to New York City and would be passing through nearby Ridgefield, Connecticut. He immediately raised a group of one hundred volunteers who were ready to fight the rearguard of the retreating redcoats. Although the rebels claimed victory, it came at a high price for Arnold, who was injured when his horse was shot out from under him and landed on Arnold's left leg.

Because Arnold had distinguished himself on the

battlefield, General Washington called on him to join the battle to retake Fort Ticonderoga. Washington needed Arnold to join the Northern Department of the Continental army. Arnold demonstrated an aggressive style of command in a series of battles that turned the tide of the war in the favor of the colonists.

Benedict Arnold's involvement in the so-called Saratoga campaign was key in the rebel victory. But because of petty bickering between Arnold and Major General Horatio Gates, who found Arnold to be a "pompous little fellow," he was left out of the final battle plans. But Arnold would not let Gates stop him from serving his army. Without receiving any orders to act, Arnold entered the battle and rallied the American troops. At day's end, British general John Burgoyne—out of supplies and cut off from retreat—realized that he had no choice but to surrender.

What should have been a proud day for Arnold turned into an insult. General Gates relieved Arnold of his command and gave him no credit for his role in the victory. In fact, Gates soundly criticized Arnold for disobeying orders and exceeding his authority.

During the Saratoga campaign, Arnold had once again injured his leg. The damage was so severe that doctors considered amputating it. Arnold would have no part of that. Instead, he spent a few months in the hospital wracked with horrible pain. When he was discharged from the hospital, Arnold was permanently scarred and his left leg was two inches shorter than his right. Despite his injury, Arnold spent the winter of 1777–1778 with the Continental army in Valley Forge, Pennsylvania, enduring the grim hardships of that wretched season.

Although Arnold's battlefield heroics were the stuff of legend, he was dogged by rumors and gossip about his behavior: that he had let smallpox spread through the American camp in Quebec, that he had mismanaged the fleet on Lake Champlain, and that he had exhibited poor judgment and character by earning money from business schemes while he was in the army. Arnold's promotion by Congress to major general did little to diminish his resentment. Not only did he feel that he should have been promoted sooner; he also felt that he should have received a higher rank. When Congress later recommended that he be court-martialed for some of his money-making schemes, Arnold saw himself as the victim of the judgments of incompetents who'd never seen battle.

Benedict Arnold's fortunes—though not his resentments—changed in June 1778, when he was appointed military commander of Philadelphia. He immediately moved into a sumptuous mansion and decorated it with costly furnishings. He threw lavish parties, always serving the finest food and drink. As Arnold spent more and more money, the government was building its court-martial case against him.

Not long after his marriage to Peggy Shippen, daughter

of a prominent Philadelphia Loyalist and nearly twenty years his junior, he was court-martialed. The charge: questionable practices as military governor, such as having a friend set up a company that bought supplies the army would need, then sold them to the army at inflated prices, turning a tidy profit for General Arnold and himself.

The trial was long and difficult for Arnold, but in the end he felt vindicated when he was acquitted. While four of the presiding officers wanted Arnold discharged from the army, it was determined that his punishment would be a reprimand from the commander in chief.

Benedict Arnold was angry and disgusted with the treatment he had received. So it came as no surprise to his wife that, in early May 1779, he secretly offered his services to the British. In fact, she may have encouraged his treasonous actions. Although the negotiations with the British took over a year, a deal was finally struck. Arnold would gain command of the garrison at West Point, New York, and then surrender the fort and its three thousand soldiers to the British. In return, he would receive a comparable rank in the British army and receive a cash payment equivalent to about one million dollars today.

Benedict Arnold began to act with the cunning of an espionage agent. He sent word to General Wilhelm von Knyphausen, the acting British commander in New York, that he was prepared to "undertake the part in question." However, Arnold wanted to make sure he and his mission were protected. He asked for a "small sum of ready money." Further, he wanted to make sure that the field agent he would meet was authentic. Von Knyphausen gave Arnold a ring, informing him that he should trust only an agent who wore an identical ring.

Not satisfied with betraying the rebel cause, Arnold also began spying for the British. Using the code name Mr. Moore, he wrote to British general Henry Clinton revealing Washington's plans to invade Canada and to add six thousand troops to his force of four thousand. Arnold also informed Clinton that, although Arnold had not yet received the command of West Point, it was only a matter of time before he took over the strategically crucial garrison. Arnold confided in the British general that he had "a drawing of the works on both sides of the river done by a French engineer." With this map, Arnold assured Clinton, the British "might take [West Point] without loss."

Like many spies, Benedict Arnold sent his military intelligence in secret code. His code used *Blackstone's Commentaries*, a classic legal book, as a codebook. He had sent a copy of this book to Clinton with directions on how they would use it to communicate. Each word in their messages would be found in the pages of *Blackstone's* and encoded with a number that would indicate the page number, the column on that page, and the place in the column for that word. For example, the word *garrison* might be encoded as *3520216,* indicating that the word appeared on page 352, in the right-hand column (*01* would indicate the left-hand column), and sixteen words from the top of that column. Arnold soon abandoned *Blackstone's* in favor of a best-selling English dictionary with words listed alphabetically, making the encoding and decoding processes much easier.

In the meantime, Arnold continued to lobby George Washington for command of West Point, which he considered the "key to America," because if the British controlled West Point, they could effectively drive a wedge between the two wings of the Continental army. Although Washington had other plans for Arnold, he issued new orders, notifying Arnold that he was to "proceed to West Point and take command of that post and its dependencies."

Benedict Arnold wasted no time putting his treacherous plan into motion. Anxious to deliver more useful intelligence to General Clinton, Arnold tried to penetrate the American spy network. He wrote to American general Robert Howe and to General Lafayette, asking for the names of the spies that they had used. There was nothing suspicious about such a request. It was common practice for a new commander to have this information so he could continue using the operatives.

However, both generals turned down his request, undoubtedly saving the lives of a number of Patriot spies.

Despite this rebuff, Arnold knew it was time to meet with a British officer who had the authority to approve final plans for the surrender of West Point. Arnold, changing his code name to Monk, began a coded communication with Mr. John Anderson, the code name for Major John André, Clinton's adjutant general. Arnold wanted "Mr. Anderson" to come "mysteriously" and meet with him. André supported such a meeting because he wanted to finally meet the man who had provided such valuable intelligence.

André's first attempt to meet with Arnold was aborted when the American patrol boats in the Hudson River fired on André's ship, the HMS *Vulture*. Arnold had failed to notify the gunships that the *Vulture* would be arriving under a flag of truce. With a keen sense of disappointment, André returned to give the news to Clinton.

Ten days passed before André made another attempt to meet with Arnold. This trip seemed ill fated from the start. First, André disregarded Clinton's warning about not traveling at night. His ship anchored in a safe spot, and he was carried upriver in a small boat. However, by the time he reached the meeting place, six miles from the *Vulture,* it was nearly two o'clock in the morning. He and Arnold would barely have two hours to discuss their deal before daylight. While there

General Benedict Arnold and Major John André meet on the banks of the Hudson River.

is no record of the particulars they discussed, they obviously reached an agreement on the betrayal. While Major André never got to give his side of the story, Arnold had this to say:

> *[Major André] was so fully convinced of the reasonableness of my proposal of being allowed 10,000 pounds sterling for my services, risks, and the loss*

which I should sustain in case of a discovery of my
plans should oblige me to take refuge in New York
before it could be fully carried into execution, that he
assured me, though he was commissioned to prom-
ise me only 6,000 pounds sterling, he would use his
influence to recommend it to your Excellency.

Arnold needed to return to the garrison at West Point, so he left André in the care of Joshua Hett Smith, one of his associates. Smith accompanied André back to the river's edge. However, the farmers who had rowed André upriver refused to take him back downriver to the *Vulture* because they feared traveling in daylight in plain sight of the cannons on the other side of the river. When Smith realized that no amount of arguing would change the farmers' decision, he and "Mr. Anderson" climbed on horses and raced the six miles to the *Vulture*.

Despite Arnold's direct order to Colonel Henry Livingston, commander of the heavy guns at Teller's Point, not to open fire, Livingston panicked at the sight of the *Vulture*. If he didn't fire, he reasoned, what would stop Loyalists in the area from rowing out to the ship and plotting mayhem? A two-hour gun battle ensued. Despite efforts to move the *Vulture* out of range, the ship was pounded. However, the ship did manage to score a hit on Livingston's powder magazine. She then slipped downriver.

André wanted to wait for the *Vulture*'s return, but Smith advised against it, arguing that the ship was unlikely to risk more enemy fire. André decided to return to the British lines on horseback—an extremely risky venture.

No one knows why André decided at this point to exchange his uniform for civilian clothes, but for whatever reason, André took off his uniform coat and slipped into a burgundy coat with gold-laced buttons and buttonholes that Smith had brought. In addition, he wore a yellow cotton waistcoat and breeches, but he retained his shiny white-topped riding boots. Over all this he wore his own blue cape. André knew that, with that change of clothes, death on the gallows was inescapable if he were caught. Had he remained in uniform, he would have been treated as a prisoner of war, with the protections that come with that designation.

To further seal his fate, Major André jammed the papers he had gotten from Arnold into one of his boots. When Arnold had warned him to dispose of the papers if he were caught, André told him that he would throw them overboard. But now, André was traveling on horseback over the roads of New York, where safely disposing of the papers presented more of a problem.

These incriminating papers contained pieces of military intelligence, including a summary of the Continental army's strength and a report about the number of troops that the British would need to have at West Point and other area defenses. In addition, they included a report from Arnold on the weapons at West Point and the plan of cannon installations in case of an attack. Finally, the papers included a copy of the minutes from a Council of War meeting of September 6 that Washington had sent Arnold, as well as Arnold's own report of the defensive shortcomings at West Point. Indeed, André's boot was filled with information enough to hang him and Arnold as well, since many of the notes were in the traitor's handwriting.

Major John André is captured on his way back to the British lines.

The final scene of Major John André's undoing began the following morning, September 23, as he approached Tarrytown, New York. Three men, who were set to rob him, accosted him at gunpoint. The major thought these men were Tories and said, "Gentlemen, I hope you belong to our party." "What party?" one of the highwaymen asked. When André told them that he meant the British, the men assured him that they were, indeed, loyal to the king. Relieved, André quickly told the men that he was a British officer and he could not be detained. His relief turned to shock when the men replied that they were Americans and he was their prisoner.

Because of the evidence against him—traveling in civilian clothes, bearing a false name, and carrying military intelligence—Major André was condemned by Washington to be hanged as a spy. Sir Henry Clinton, quite fond of his adjutant, did almost everything he could to secure André's release. What he would not do, however, was swap André for Benedict Arnold, who had fled to New York after he had gotten word of André's capture. Washington stood firm in his decision. In fact, when Clinton requested that André be given a soldier's execution by firing squad, Washington refused. On October 2, 1780, Major John André was hanged.

As for the scoundrel in all this, Benedict Arnold found a lukewarm welcome among the British soldiers. He was given the rank of brigadier general and commanded a regiment that raided supply depots in New London, Connecticut, and Richmond, Virginia. In fact, it was Arnold's men who burned Richmond during one of their raids. Arnold was particularly brutal to the civilians in his path, burning ships and grain supplies.

General Washington was so incensed by Arnold's betrayal—personally and militarily—that he approved a plan to kidnap the traitor and bring him to trial. However, circumstances never permitted the American agents to get close enough to Arnold to nab him. In late 1781, Benedict Arnold sailed to England; he spent the remaining years of his life in poor health, shunned by the people he thought would consider him a hero.

By the time the American Revolution officially ended in 1783 with the Treaty of Paris, the young American government had made strides in espionage operations. However, the new nation had more pressing business to deal with than the development of an intelligence agency. It took a major national crisis—the Civil War—to force the government and the military to think again about espionage.

Invisible Ink

WE'VE SEEN HOW THE CULPER SPY RING made effective use of coded messages. They also used another trick: invisible ink. The ink they used—most commonly referred to as stain and also known as white ink or sympathetic ink—was developed in England, of all places, by Sir James Jay, brother of the Patriot John Jay. This special ink disappeared when used on white paper. An agent would later brush a developer—frequently sodium carbonate (baking soda)—over the writing, and the message would reappear. What was in the stain? The formula remains unknown.

Having a good invisible ink can make it easier to send intelligence. However, using it in a clever way is also important. At first, agents simply wrote their messages with stain on a blank sheet of white paper, then sent it off by courier. General Washington soon realized that a blank sheet of paper would arouse suspicions if it fell into the wrong hands, so he offered some recommendations to his agents who sent messages in invisible ink. They included:

- Write messages on the pages of a pamphlet or on the first few pages of a common pocket notebook, on the blank pages at the end of an almanac, or in "any publication of small value."

- Write a friendly letter in regular ink, but add intelligence in stain between the lines of these letters.
- Fold the letters in a particular way to alert the recipients of the stain contents.
- Write a brief letter and use the remainder of the sheet of paper for secret intelligence.

Culper Jr. devised his own method of hiding a secret message in packages of writing paper that he shipped to his customers on Long Island, including Culper Sr. Culper Jr. wrote his messages in stain on one of the sheets of paper, then slipped it into the package of sheets in a predetermined spot, say the thirtieth sheet from the bottom. When his partner received the shipment of paper, he simply counted to the thirtieth sheet from the bottom and found the sheet with the secret message on it.

The rebels were not the only ones using invisible ink to keep their intelligence messages hidden from the enemy. Major John André told British secret agents to mark correspondence written in invisible ink with an *F* (for *fire*) if it was to be developed by heat and an *A* (for *acid*) if the reader should use some sort of chemical solution. No matter which method the agents used, all needed to exercise care in handling invisible ink letters because water or other liquids would easily smear the secret writing and make it unreadable.

A page of a letter written in invisible ink by Major John André to General Henry Clinton. Note the A (for acid) in the upper right-hand corner, indicating that the letter can be developed with a developing agent.

To further conceal intelligence, couriers needed to hide their secret messages in the event they were stopped. Messages were sewn inside of buttons and hidden in small silver balls that were made of two hollow halves.

When Daniel Taylor, a British spy carrying a message in a silver capsule, was stopped by rebels, he quickly popped it into his mouth and swallowed it. The rebels gave Taylor a hearty dose of a vomit-inducing potion, which did its work. But Taylor grabbed the ball and swallowed it again. When the American general informed the spy that the rebels would hang him and cut the silver ball out of his stomach, Taylor agreed to a second dose of the potion. The rebels found the military intelligence in the capsule and hanged him anyway on October 16, 1777, after a court-martial.

Spies in Blue and Gray

When the first shot of the Civil War was fired at four thirty in the morning on April 12, 1861, many believed that it would be a short conflict. Even though Fort Sumter had to endure thirty-four hours of Confederate bombardment before the Union surrendered it, the Union enjoyed a number of significant advantages over the Confederacy. Yet, by the time Robert E. Lee surrendered to Ulysses Grant at Appomattox, Virginia, some four years later, about 620,000 soldiers had died on the battlefields, more than American battle deaths in all other wars from the Revolution through the Vietnam War.

Most of the war was fought in states south of Washington, D.C., so Southerners saw the Union army as an invading force. For the Union soldiers, this meant they had to fight in unfamiliar and hostile territory. This matter of geography affected the spies who worked behind enemy lines. Northern spies could not often count on much hospitality from Southerners. On the other hand, since so much of the war was fought in the South, Confederate spies could usually find a safe house, or at least a sympathetic soul who was willing to allow a "good southern boy" to hide in their barn until the danger had passed.

Just as in the Revolutionary War, most of the spies of the Civil War were amateurs. The United States government had not developed any systematic framework for gathering military intelligence in the nine decades since the Revolution. By some accounts, there were thousands of amateur spies at work during the early years of the Civil War. The spy game at that point was very much a vocation that relied upon on-the-job training. And, since neither side had any significant experience in the areas of intelligence gathering and counterintelligence, spying was, in a sense, easy for both sides. With no counterintelligence system, the chances of getting caught were low. Things tightened up as the war progressed, when some spies were caught and executed. But, as in other wars, the fear of capture and death did little to deter the intrepid spy.

Another thing that changed very little in the years between the wars was the means of obtaining military intelligence. Although the use of photography and the telegraph brought some technological advances, the craft of spying on the enemy's army still relied on fieldwork. For the most part, intelligence was gathered in simple ways. Prisoners of war and deserters were interrogated. The Union army was always interested in hearing what runaway slaves had to report. And, of course, both armies relied on cavalry scouts, signal intercepts, visual observation, and captured correspondence.

One of the main functions of the cavalry was reconnaissance. When it was impractical to send a cavalry unit to gather intelligence, a division commander might send an individual scout or a small scouting party. Scouts made visual observation of troop placement and movements and also intercepted messages sent from elevated signal stations. Later in the war, observation balloons also began to be used for intelligence gathering.

Another valuable source of intelligence, which may seem hard to fathom for us in our world of e-mails, instant messages, and cell phones, was enemy newspapers. Field commanders always felt fortunate when they could get their hands on a recent newspaper from enemy territory. News reports might contain information about troop movements, recruitment, and transportation disruptions. However, as valuable as some of this intelligence might be, it was worthless if it arrived too late to be helpful.

Spies in the Civil War, particularly Confederate spies, relied on courier systems to help speed their information to battlefield generals. Often these courier systems included female operatives. In fact, the Civil War saw an increase in the number of women involved in espionage, a few gaining legendary status in the process.

Elizabeth Van Lew

Elizabeth Van Lew was a quiet aristocratic woman who was not afraid to take a firm stand against slavery and secession. More important for the Union war effort, she was destined to become one of the most successful and productive spies in the war.

Elizabeth Van Lew was born in 1818 to upper-class parents who were raised in the North. They settled in Richmond, Virginia—destined to become the capital of the Confederate States of America—where Elizabeth spent nearly her entire life. But in the early 1830s, Elizabeth was sent to live with her relatives in Philadelphia, where she attended the same private academy that her mother, Eliza, had attended. More than likely it was while she attended school in Philadelphia

Elizabeth Van Lew, Union spymaster

that she heard much of the talk about the abolitionist movement. One historian believes that the young girl had a governess who spoke to her of the need to emancipate the slaves. By the time she returned to her family's Richmond mansion, Van Lew had a strong and growing belief that slavery was immoral. As she wrote in her journal, "Slave power is arrogant—is jealous, and intrusive—is cruel—is despotic." Because of her abolitionist views, Van Lew was shunned by many in her social circle, writing in her journal that she felt as if she and her family were "plague-stricken."

When the war began, Elizabeth Van Lew was considered a southern "spinster." She was in her early forties and unmarried. What could she do, she wondered, to serve her country? The answer came to her when she recalled her father's aunt Letitia telling her how she had ministered to the captured troops of the Continental army during the American Revolution, especially those who had been wounded in action.

But Elizabeth wanted to do more than simply minister and comfort the wounded. A Unionist, believing in "one nation . . . indivisible," she *needed* to do more. When she learned of Virginia's secession from the Union in 1861, she felt, in the words of one historian, "profoundly betrayed." She believed that the secessionists did not represent the majority of the citizens of Virginia. She was compelled to act in any way she could to help repair a nation torn apart.

Elizabeth Van Lew decided she would carry on the tradition of her great-aunt by caring for federal troops imprisoned in Richmond. In 1862, nearly 50,000 prisoners were kept in Libby Prison, a converted warehouse six blocks or so from the Van Lew home on Church Hill.

At first, Van Lew's scheme was rejected, when Brigadier General John H. Winder, inspector general of military camps for Richmond, denied her permission to enter the prison. She was, however, allowed to visit injured Yankee soldiers in the prison hospital. One soldier noted in his journal that "she alone went from cot to cot where lay a sufferer in blue." She did what she could for the wounded soldiers, bringing them messages and money, and no small amount of food.

In hushed tones, she talked to the men about where they had been and what they had seen and heard. The more she listened to the prisoners, the more she realized that they possessed information that could be of value to the Union army. Alert federal soldiers took notice of rebel troop strength and movement. They recognized who commanded which rebel armies. Overhearing conversations of the Confederates who captured and transported them to prison often offered insight into the morale of the rebel troops. As any good spy will do, Van Lew listened attentively to the information the soldiers provided, and then, with the help of the Richmond underground, she passed it on to Union army commanders.

No one in Libby Prison hospital paid much attention to this tiny, birdlike woman with a thin nose and alert blue eyes as she went about her business of visiting the hospitalized soldiers. She read to them and brought them baskets of goodies. The Confederate guards had no idea that this kindhearted woman was gathering military intelligence from the prisoners and laying the groundwork for espionage activities.

Realizing that they could do more if they banded together, groups of the Richmond Unionists began to organize. As Van Lew built stronger relationships with wounded soldiers, the Unionists made plans to hide Union soldiers who escaped from Libby Prison. In fact, the Van Lew mansion became a primary safe house, a place where escaped prisoners would be hidden and cared for. Elizabeth, her mother, and their servants did all they could to prepare the escaped soldiers for the treacherous journey behind enemy lines as they attempted to rejoin their fellow soldiers. The Unionists well understood that every escapee was a potential source of valuable military intelligence, and they made certain that each soldier was debriefed before starting back to the Union lines.

The use of the Church Hill mansion emboldened Van Lew. She was ready to take a more active role in the service of her country. Her official recruitment as a spy came late in 1863. In November, General Benjamin Butler was placed in charge of the Department of Virginia and North Carolina, putting him in command of much of the area of eastern Virginia, which included directing the Army of the James against Richmond. He was savvy enough to realize that any chance he had of capturing Richmond would be significantly improved if he received inside help from Richmond Unionists. If they could provide him with accurate intelligence, he and his troops would take care of the rest. Butler needed a "correspondent in Richmond," as he put it to a friend.

On December 8, 1863, two Union soldiers, Harry Catlin and John R. McCullough, escaped from the Libby Prison hospital. The Richmond newspaper carried details of the audacious escape. This was a propaganda triumph for the Richmond Unionists that infuriated Southerners who couldn't believe that villainous Yankee sympathizers lived among them.

Ten days after the escape, McCullough reached the Union camp. In the intervening days, he helped the underground in its espionage activities, passing along information about General Lee's recruiting efforts in Richmond and about Confederate shortages of staples such as sugar and coffee, as well as iron, which was needed for the manufacture of ammunition. When McCullough finally met with General Butler, he told him about the operations of the Richmond Unionists, especially the work of Elizabeth Van Lew. From that discussion, Van Lew met with General Butler at William Rowley's farmhouse a few miles south of Richmond, one of five safe houses that were especially comforting to the Union couriers and escapees. At Rowley's house, Butler explained that he required, as he had put it in an earlier letter, a person who could "write me of course without name or description of the writer, and . . . only incur the risk of dropping an ordinary letter by flag of truce in the Post Office, directed to a name at the North." (Both the Union and the Confederacy had agreed to permit the uninterrupted flow of mail between civilians, be they Northerner or Southerner.) Van Lew would need to write her secret messages in invisible ink. She was to write her message in the space between the lines of an innocuous letter that a "dear aunt" might write.

Armed with invisible ink, a cipher system, and a passion to end the war and preserve the Union, Elizabeth Van Lew became Butler's eyes and ears in the Confederate capital city. Truth be told, however, she became much more than that. She became a spymaster, the person responsible for running a network of agents, couriers, and safe houses that was very active during the war. In addition to the spying, Elizabeth Van Lew continued to maintain her Church Hill home as a safe house and something of a local Union spy headquarters.

It may seem surprising that no Confederate sympathizers took action against Van Lew, given her strong and public views on secession and slavery. Surely there were suspicions, especially among her upper-crust neighbors, but the matter never went beyond those suspicions. Historians have suggested that the secessionists were victims of their own cultural bias, believing that no aristocratic person, and certainly not a lady, would ever consider taking part in anything as impolite as spying. A true lady managed her servants, prepared parties and gatherings, and blindly supported her husband. Such attitudes worked in Van Lew's favor, diverting suspicion from her.

Van Lew continued to be alert to any helpful information she was able to overhear when she visited the prisoners. The guards were often careless in their speech when Van Lew was within earshot. She instructed her operatives to be on the lookout for loose-lipped soldiers who might unwisely let slip a tidbit of military intelligence. By the summer of 1864, she was sending her handler about three messages per week, filled with news of troop movement, supply shortages, and the psychological state of the soldiers as well as of Richmond's citizens.

To assure that the intelligence reached the commanders as quickly as possible—the postal services having become slow and unreliable—Van Lew created a system of couriers that moved the intelligence on its way without burdening one operative with the responsibility (and danger) of making the entire trip. She also created a credible cover story for each of her couriers, should they be stopped and questioned along the way.

In addition, Van Lew did not hesitate to use her servants

as couriers, once again taking advantage of a Southern attitude (shared, unfortunately, by many Northerners as well)—in this case, that blacks were too slow-witted to be part of an espionage ring. For their part, the servants, well aware of what was at stake in the war, were eager to assist Van Lew in any way they could. One servant, for example, carrying a basket of eggs along a country road was not apt to arouse any curiosity. However, hidden among the fresh eggs was one hollowed-out egg that held a secret message. A black seamstress would hide the intelligence among the paper dress patterns she carried with her sewing supplies. The guards at Libby Prison were used to seeing black servants bring food and other items to the prisoners, unaware that the servants were also swapping information with them. One of the Van Lew servants was often sent with a plate of homemade food on a lovely family platter; the platter had a false bottom that was meant to hold hot water to keep the food warm. Van Lew, however, used that space to hide her secret messages.

When the campaign around Richmond intensified, the prison commandant clamped down on visitors, forbidding any conversation during visits. Undeterred by the strict prison rules, Van Lew found ways to continue her intelligence swap with the prisoners. She realized, for example, that the books she frequently brought for the prisoners could offer a variety of ways to exchange information. She could tuck enciphered messages down a book's spine. She also developed another way of using books to conceal secret messages. She opened a book to a prearranged page and made a pinhole above each letter on that page that spelled out her secret message. Prisoners could easily respond in the same way.

In addition to getting valuable military intelligence from Union soldiers, Elizabeth Van Lew and the Richmond underground helped them plan escapes. Van Lew knew that, in addition to freeing soldiers and officers to continue to fight for the Union, escapes were also valuable propaganda for the Richmond newspapers. She and her agents helped a number of soldiers escape, but no escape was more spectacular than the 1864 escape of more than 109 soldiers from Libby Prison.

The escape was the brainchild of Colonel Thomas E. Rose and Major Andrew G. Hamilton, who were captured in the Tennessee campaign of September 1863. These officers organized a small team of prisoners to dig an escape tunnel. Over the next seven months, the diggers made three attempts to complete the tunnel without success. The first tunnel flooded with water from a nearby canal. The second collapsed. They then attempted to connect the third tunnel to a sewer line, but found that the sewer was too narrow to use for passage.

Early in February 1864, the diggers thought they had dug far enough, but they discovered that the tunnel exit hole was still in the line of vision of the guard tower. After making a few calculations, Rose decided that they needed to shift the digging more to the left. On the night of February 9, they broke through the ground again and discovered that they were exactly where they'd wanted to be: in a tobacco shack that was hidden from the guards by a plank fence. Under

cover of night, they made their way to prearranged Unionist safe houses, including the home of Elizabeth Van Lew.

Prison officials were furious when morning roll call revealed the escape. But they reacted quickly and sent messengers in every direction to notify rebel pickets of the escape.

A stereograph of the old Libby Prison, Richmond, Virginia

More guards were placed on bridges and on the roads in the area around Richmond. About half of the escapees were captured, returned to Libby Prison, and immediately placed in chains in "narrow and loathsome" cells, with nothing but bread and water. Robert Ford, who took care of the prison's horses and was a Unionist, was treated viciously for his role in aiding the prisoners who escaped. He received five hundred lashes and was whipped "nearly to death."

About fifty-five Union soldiers remained free and were able to return to their fighting units. Elizabeth Van Lew and the underground worked together to pass on intelligence about the escape. Union sympathizers were very pleased with the propaganda victory that was achieved by the escape. People in Richmond would not soon forget the "Great Yankee Wonder."

The last few years of Van Lew's life were not happy years. Her brother and sister died in 1895. But by far the worst loss was the unexpected death in May 1900 of her beloved niece, Eliza, whom Elizabeth had treated like her daughter. Elizabeth Van Lew died four months later at the age of eighty-two and was buried vertically rather than horizontally because of the limited space remaining in the family cemetery plot.

In death, as in the last years of her life, her benefactors saw to it that Elizabeth Van Lew received the honor she deserved. A boulder was shipped from the grounds of the

State House in Boston to the Shockoe Cemetery in Richmond. The stone bore a bronze panel that said, in part, that:

SHE RISKED EVERYTHING THAT IS DEAR TO MAN—FRIENDS—FORTUNE—COMFORT— HEALTH—LIFE ITSELF—ALL FOR THE ONE ABSORBING DESIRE OF HER HEART—THAT SLAVERY MIGHT BE ABOLISHED AND THE UNION PRESERVED

From Clotheslines to Balloons

THE CIVIL WAR did bring a few technological advances that began to change the way intelligence could be gathered and reported. Although largely untested, observation balloons and the telegraph were first used for gathering intelligence during the Civil War. The overall effect of this new technology on the war was not significant. Nonetheless, each of these innovations was only at the start of its place in espionage and intelligence gathering. Each developed further in subsequent wars.

The first balloon flight in time of war lifted off the ground on June 18, 1861, in a test flight over Washington, D.C. The balloon, carrying Thaddeus S. C. Lowe, rose five hundred feet—about as high as a fifty-story building—and hovered over the capital. A transmission cable ran from the balloon's gondola to the office of the War Department, and Lowe earned a place in history for initiating the first wartime air-to-ground communication ever recorded in America. His demonstration introduced the generals to a breakthrough tool of aerial reconnaissance for gathering intelligence in real time. Lincoln was sold on the idea of spying from the sky. He ordered his commander in chief, General Winfield Scott, to organize a Balloon Corps with Lowe as its chief aeronaut.

Lowe wound up making espionage flights over Yorktown, Virginia, as well as over other battles in the state during the Peninsular campaign of 1862. After flying a balloon named *Intrepid* over the battle of Fair Oaks, he returned with timely intelligence that allowed General Samuel Heintzelman to escape an approaching Confederate army. Other flights provided generals and mapmakers with intelligence that helped them draw maps of enemy fortifications. On another flight over Richmond, Lowe brought a map with him and marked Confederate positions in red.

The rebels, of course, tried to shoot down the balloons, without success. Musket fire did not have the range to hit a balloon. And they learned that cannon fire had a trajectory that was far better suited for ground-to-ground firing than ground-to-air firing. The rebels soon realized that by firing on the balloons, they were merely calling attention to their own positions.

The rebels did soon figure out some ways to reduce the success of the balloonist spies. They camouflaged their camps with tree branches, and they also blacked out the camps at night, forbidding campfires, so the spies hovering above could not make an accurate estimate of troop strength. In addition, they painted logs black and set them up to look like cannons from a thousand feet above. These fakes were dubbed Quaker guns.

The rebels did launch their own balloon program, but it struggled with technological problems. For one thing, their aeronauts had trouble controlling their balloons once they were aloft, a problem that Lowe had solved for the Union army balloons by tethering the balloon to a steam locomotive, which pulled it to an advantageous site. The Confederates attempted to have a tugboat pull a balloon down the James River, but this plan flopped when the tug ran aground on a sandbar and Union soldiers soon captured both the boat and the balloon. While the balloon flights by both sides in the war were of historical importance, their impact on the war was minimal.

The biggest technological advance in the intelligence arena was the use of the telegraph, which enabled field commanders to quickly communicate with other commanders and with the War Department. It was not out of the ordinary that 4,500 messages, usually encrypted and some as long as a thousand words, passed between the War Department and the Union commanders each day. More than anything else, speed of communication over many miles was the most important strategic advantage of the telegraph. And, since intelligence becomes useless if it is not received in a timely manner, the speed of telegraph messages was a significant military advance.

But like most technological advances, the telegraph brought its own problems—the most obvious stemming from the fact that a telegraph system needed wooden poles with transmission wires strung between them. Poles were cut down and burned. Wires were cut. It proved impossible to guard the

The U.S. spy balloon Intrepid *lifts off.*

many miles of telegraph lines from the work of saboteurs. And, of course, telegraph wires could be (and were) tapped, allowing each side to read the other's messages. Before long, both sides realized that a more successful tactic was to capture an enemy telegraph station. Such a takeover not only allowed soldiers to intercept every message, but it also gave them the chance to send out disinformation using the enemy's own telegraph wires.

The Union Army did try to make their telegraphic messages more secure by enciphering them using what is called a route transposition. In such a system, the message to be sent was written in a grid of, say five rows and five columns for a message of twenty-five words. So the grid below would be used to send the message: *Be advised that the troops of the enemy forces will pass by the valley in two days. Prepare to meet them no later than sunrise.*

BE	ADVISED	THAT	THE	TROOPS
OF	THE	ENEMY	FORCES	WILL
PASS	BY	THE	VALLEY	IN
TWO	DAYS.	PREPARE	TO	MEET
THEM	NO	LATER	THAN	SUNRISE.

The enciphered message was then sent by telegraph using columns rather than rows and look like this: *be of pass two them advised by the days no that enemy the prepare later the forces valley to than troops will in meet sunrise.* When the message arrived at its destination, the receiver knew to write it out in a five-by-five grid to read the secret message.

Despite its shortcomings, the telegraph was a huge improvement over the flags and torches used earlier by army signalizers. A signalizer sent messages using a wigwag system, which was a two-part enciphering system created by a Union medical officer. A signalizer would move a flag or a light to the left for *1*, to the right for *2*. Each letter was represented by a combination of left and right movements. For example, the letter *T* might be sent as *2122*. Or right-left-right-right. Such messages were obviously insecure, easily seen by other signalizers scanning the horizon for the sender. While cipher systems were used in messages, they were generally elementary and easily deciphered by signalizers on either side.

The "clothesline" code used by the Culper spy ring during the Revolutionary War was also used in the Civil War. Union sympathizers might, for example, hang three shirts on a clothesline to indicate to Union agents that the local rebel army had been reinforced. An empty line, on the other hand might mean that the rebels had withdrawn from the area. Related to this simple system was the "window-shade" code in which a raised and lowered window shade at a particular window would really be a message sent to a watching signalizer.

Rose O'Neale Greenhow

Like Elizabeth Van Lew, Rose O'Neale Greenhow drew praise from one side of the Mason-Dixon Line and revulsion from the other side for her espionage activities. Her supporters in the Confederacy called her Wild Rose, in admiration of her espionage exploits. Northerners, appalled by the treachery of this Washington socialite, called her Rebel Rose. Regardless of the feelings for Greenhow, it is difficult to ignore the espionage work she did for the cause she supported.

Rose O'Neale Greenhow loved the social life of prewar Washington, D.C. Like Elizabeth Van Lew, she moved in upper-class social circles. She was disappointed when she had to leave the excitement of Washington to follow her husband, Robert Greenhow Jr. He had served for twenty years as a translator and librarian at the State Department but took a job in San Francisco, working for the California Land Commission.

Although San Francisco offered some of the amenities of the nation's capital, Rose O'Neale Greenhow's life took a tragic turn on February 17, 1854, when her husband fell from a wooden sidewalk to the ground six feet below. Robert Greenhow suffered a broken leg and internal injuries; he then probably developed an infection as well. He lingered in and out of consciousness until he died on March 27, six weeks after his fall.

Rose O'Neale Greenhow, Confederate spy

Rose O'Neale Greenhow, a widow at forty, returned to Washington to resume the social life that she had left. She quickly learned, however, that things had changed as the divided nation had gone to war. While many men in positions of responsibility in the government and in the military left the capital to fight for the Confederacy, some remained. One Confederate sympathizer who remained in Washington was Captain Thomas Jordan. On the staff of Union general Winfield Scott, Jordan was the officer responsible for drawing up the initial war plans used against the Confederacy. Jordan had one reason for wanting to remain with Scott as long as he could: to learn more about the battle strategy of the Union army. In addition to reading Scott's battle plans,

Jordan established a spy network of some fifty agents. Some had espionage experience, but most were amateurs.

Rose O'Neale Greenhow was one such amateur recruited by Jordan. Greenhow, in fact, became the spymaster for a band of Confederate agents. She had the qualities that Jordan was looking for: an intense dislike of Northerners and their attempt to impose their will on the established Southern culture, as well as complete disdain for anyone—particularly Northerners—who wanted to abolish slavery. In addition, like Elizabeth Van Lew, she held fast to her convictions and was not afraid to speak her mind about them.

Jordan taught Greenhow a very basic substitution cipher, in which a letter, symbol, or number stood for a different letter or, in some cases, an entire word. For example, *Z* might stand for *C*—or for *troops* or *railroad station*. The new Confederate spymaster spent hours practicing her enciphering skills. She soon turned her Sixteenth Street house in Washington into the unofficial headquarters of her espionage ring. The spies who worked with her supplied intelligence about troop movements in and around Washington. Some were adept at getting intelligence from people in the U.S. government.

By some accounts, Rose O'Neale Greenhow was considered "irresistible." She was quick to use her appearance to attract men, although she wasn't interested in just *any* man. She was only interested in men who could furnish information that might aid the Confederacy.

One such man was Senator Henry Wilson of Massachusetts, chairman of the Senate Military Affairs Committee. As the prospect of war grew, Greenhow did her best to cultivate her relationship with Wilson without tipping her hand about her secessionist allegiance. In her autobiography, Greenhow claimed that Wilson wanted to marry her. Although she also claimed that he furnished her with military intelligence, there is no solid proof that supports her assertion.

There is evidence, however, that one piece of intelligence Greenhow passed on—one based on her own observations in Washington—had a significant effect on the war. On July 10, 1861, she sent an enciphered message to Confederate general Pierre Beauregard, informing him that General Irvin McDowell, commander of the Army of Northeastern Virginia, had been ordered to march on Richmond and that he would be leaving Washington in sixteen days. Beauregard sent a courier to confirm the message. The courier returned with Greenhow's confirming enciphered message hidden in the hollowed-out heel of his boot: *Order issued for McDowell to march upon Manassas tonight.*

Beauregard moved his troops into position and surprised McDowell at Bull Run Creek, near Manassas, soundly thrashing the Union army. The defeat was devastating to the Northern war effort. Many in the North had thought that the war would be over in a short time, but the crushing defeat at Bull Run showed them otherwise. On the other hand, the Confederate victory against a superior foe made the secessionists in Washington jubilant, believing that the rebel army would soon be marching down Pennsylvania Avenue.

Some historians are not sure of Greenhow's influence on the Battle of Bull Run. They point to the fact that Beauregard did not call for reinforcements until after his troops were pushed back by federal troops. It is possible that Beauregard disregarded Greenhow's message, found himself and his troops in serious trouble, and then sent a frantic call to General Joseph E. Johnston for help. By giving Greenhow credit for her intelligence—and the stunning victory—Beauregard may have been playing the Southern gentleman while covering up his blunder.

In any case, after Manassas, Greenhow received congratulations from Jordan, who wrote: "We rely upon you for further information. The Confederacy owes you a debt." Buoyed by the success at Manassas, Greenhow continued to send reports through couriers to Confederate field commanders, providing them with valuable information on troop strength, movement, and position that she would receive from her operatives who met regularly at her home. She even found some helpful information in the Washington newspapers. However, her Sixteenth Street neighbors began to grow suspicious. And unfortunately for Greenhow, they weren't the only ones who had taken note of her activities.

Allan Pinkerton, head of the Union's intelligence service and the man who would come to be "the agent of Rose's undoing," was on the case. He had his own undercover agents trying to ferret out the rebel spies working in Washington. Fortunately, Pinkerton, guilty on many occasions of seriously overestimating enemy troop strength for the government, was a better detective than military analyst. He assigned Thomas A. Scott, the new assistant secretary of war, to the case.

It didn't take Greenhow long to figure out that Pinkerton's counterintelligence net was closing around her. She developed a detailed escape plan. She spent many of her hours at home at the sewing machine, hiding secrets about Union troop movements in the lining and cuffs of her gowns. Despite feeling that her time as spymaster might end at any moment, Greenhow continued to receive military intelligence from her agents and made sure she passed it on to the field commanders, often through couriers. Because of her connection with rebel intelligence agents near Washington, she believed that the Confederacy would spirit her away to safety if the situation worsened.

However, Rose O'Neale Greenhow's luck ran out a few months after the fall of Fort Sumter. She was arrested on August 23, 1861, but was not sent to prison. Rather she was placed under house arrest, at what came to be known as Fort Greenhow. Women thought to be spies were treated differently from men by both sides. On the other hand, the fate suffered by men like John André in the Revolutionary War typified what happened to men accused of spying in the Civil War. In fact, Timothy Webster, one of Pinkerton's bright young agents, was caught spying behind enemy lines and hanged, the first such execution of the war.

Although confined to her home, Greenhow soon realized that she could learn a great deal by simply listening to the talk of her guards. Her mail was censored, but she still managed to hide secret information in innocuous-sounding letters. She also used colored yarn—what she called her "vocabulary of colour"—for sending information to rebel commanders. She wove tapestries in which military intelligence was enciphered, in a sense, in the colors of the yarn that she used. Granted, this method of transmitting intelligence was limited to very simple information, but there were times when that was all that was needed.

Before the guards made it more difficult to communicate with the rebels—Greenhow never went anywhere without a detective following close by—she wrote one of her more elaborate enciphered messages. In this message she included detailed drawings of the fortifications around Washington, as well as notes about the system's weak points. According to Greenhow, the rebels were very pleased with her drawings, which they complimented "as being equal to those of their best engineers." Rose later added, "as well they might."

In October 1861, Greenhow befriended a guard and bribed him to deliver a secret message. The guard betrayed her, however, and Pinkerton increased the guards at "Fort Greenhow." Despite Greenhow's loud and frequent complaints, Pinkerton never stopped trying to keep her from sending intelligence. At one point he put another woman prisoner in with her, hoping that Rebel Rose would incriminate herself by divulging the details of her espionage. But it didn't take Greenhow very long to figure out that the new "prisoner" was really one of Pinkerton's undercover agents.

Pinkerton next ordered that all the windows in Greenhow's home be covered with boards. Then he had all paper removed from the house. Finally, Allan Pinkerton had seen enough of what Rebel Rose could do and felt she needed to be locked up in a real prison.

She was taken to the Old Capitol Prison. Her time there was most unpleasant. She was approaching fifty, her sharp face now lined with deep wrinkles. Her cell was a mere ten by twelve feet and contained none of the finery that she was used to. Her only pieces of furniture were a straw bed and a wooden table. She was fed the same food the soldiers received. As a further indignity, her cell was infested with bedbugs and all manner of small, four-legged vermin. If prison officials expected Greenhow to give in to the rigors of her new life, they were mistaken. She behaved as she had in her life to this point. Her haughtiness did not sit well with the guards. She treated them like servants who were put there to satisfy her wants.

Greenhow found her treatment from the federal guards demeaning. Because of her fame, she was something of a tourist attraction, like a tiger in a cage. Visitors may have been surprised to find that Rebel Rose was ready to chat amicably with any of them who were so inclined. But Greenhow had only one thing on her mind during these conversations: learning any morsel of news that might help the Confederate army.

Despite all the efforts by prison officials to keep Greenhow from interacting with other prisoners, they could not completely stop her. In her autobiography, Greenhow tells of one incident that occurred when she was walking in the prison yard. Out of nowhere, a small bundle of folded paper landed at her feet. She carefully opened the paper and read that Stonewall Jackson had soundly defeated federal forces at Front Royal in the Shenandoah Valley. As Greenhow later wrote, the news "made my heart leap with joy."

After nearly ten grueling months in the Old Capitol Prison, Greenhow was set free on the last day of May in 1862. As she left the prison, she was given a warning never to return to Washington, D.C. In Richmond she took up residence in the upper-class Ballard House and soon contacted her handlers, suggesting that the rebel army take advantage of new technology by using hot-air balloons to deliver spies behind enemy lines. Soon Confederacy president Jefferson Davis made plans for her, more practical plans that he hoped would change the course of the war for the South. He wanted Rose O'Neale Greenhow to sail to Europe, to meet with heads of state in an attempt to get them to support the Confederacy, either with direct financial or material assistance or at least with a pledge that they would stay neutral in the war.

Given her love for socializing with the rich and famous, Greenhow must have been pleased with the assignment and left for London at the end of the summer of 1863. She spent a few months meeting with various British statesmen, but her requests for aid were politely rejected. Disappointed but not discouraged, she sailed across the English Channel to Paris for more negotiations. After months of spying and being con-fined to prison, Greenhow was ready to immerse herself in the gala parties in the City of Light. Despite her enjoyment of the city's social life, however, she made little progress toward getting a promise of aid from France.

Greenhow set sail for home on August 10, 1864. She brought with her gold coins that she had received as a con-tribution to the Confederacy war effort. The journey was long, but she was glad to be returning to the South. As her ship approached the eastern coast of America, however, nature

Cipher found on Greenhow's body after she drowned

conspired against her. A storm hit as the ship was preparing to run the federal blockade. Greenhow begged the captain to let her try to make it ashore in a skiff. The captain refused, but Greenhow, recalling the horrors of the Old Capitol Prison, refused to risk capture by the Union navy. She pressed her case relentlessly until the captain finally agreed to let her join a few of his sailors who would handle the skiff.

Greenhow boarded the small boat, bringing the gold coins, probably in a leather bag she had slung across her shoulders. The boat had not gone very far when it swamped and capsized. Greenhow was dragged into the sea by the weight of the gold. In the light of the next day, her body was found washed up onshore. A Confederate shore guard found the body and recovered the gold coins, for which he was given a small reward. When her body was brought to port for burial, women lined the pier in honor of Rebel Rose. Eyewitnesses reported that Rose O'Neale Greenhow looked as elegant in death as she had been in life. She was put to rest with full military honors in a local cemetery.

When Robert E. Lee surrendered his command to Ulysses S. Grant at the Appomattox courthouse in 1865, the country faced years of healing. The question of slavery would take even longer to resolve. And, although the Civil War had introduced advances in the science of war, the field of espionage made but modest gains. Perhaps the most significant was the effort by President Lincoln and his military commanders to create an organized espionage network. This legacy set the stage for better organization during America's involvement in World War I, less than fifty years after the end of the Civil War.

African Americans

THROUGHOUT THE CIVIL WAR, many African Americans were among those delivering intelligence to federal troops. The Union army was wise enough to make use of information provided by runaway slaves. General Lee believed that the Union army's "chief source of information" came from African Americans, who provided details about terrain, as well as information about hidden stores of rebel guns, supplies, and treasure. Union colonel Rush Hawkins referred to such intelligence as "Black Dispatches," and was quoted as saying, "If I want to find out anything hereabouts, I hunt up a Negro; and if he knows or can find out, I'm sure to get all I want."

Hawkins was talking about the likes of Mary Louvestre, a housekeeper for a ship's chandler near the Gosport Naval Yard in Norfolk, Virginia. She overheard her master and some navymen talking about the rebuilding of the CSS *Virginia* into an ironclad ship. If the officers at the U.S. Navy Department were surprised to hear such news, they were even more surprised—and overjoyed—when Louvestre presented them with a copy of the plans that she had stolen. With such information, the Union navy was able to speed up development of an ironclad of its own.

Without a doubt, Harriet Tubman was the most important African-American spy. Most people know Tubman as one of the foremost conductors on the Underground Railroad. In addition to helping runaway slaves escape to the North, the Underground Railroad also helped escaped Union soldiers return to their units. In fact, it was Tubman's work on the Underground Railroad that led Union generals to learn of her. When the federal General Staff recruited Harriet Tubman as a spy in 1862, she in turn recruited nine African-American men for her intelligence unit. Some of them were riverboat pilots who knew every trickle and tide of the coastal waterways.

The following year she formed a regiment of African-American soldiers under the command of Colonel James Montgomery of South Carolina. Union gunships manned by three hundred black soldiers from Tubman's regiment successfully navigated treacherous waters laced with explosive mines because intelligence from other African Americans had pinpointed the mines' locations. In enemy territory, Tubman's regiment led about eight hundred slaves to freedom and destroyed an enormous cache of food, war supplies, and cotton.

Harriet Tubman, African-American spy and conductor on the Underground Railroad.

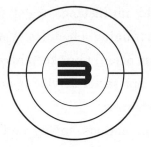

Espionage Comes of Age in World War I

At the end of the nineteenth century, spying was the business of gentlemen. It was, in a sense, conducted in the open. And because the governments of Europe had only small agencies to gather political and military information about their enemies and would-be enemies, much of the intelligence was gathered in an informal way by individuals who were not working for any intelligence agency. For example, visitors to a port city would amble about, all the while noticing what was being shipped, how much was being shipped, and where it was going. Military attachés in cities like Berlin, Vienna, and Stockholm gathered military intelligence in the country in which they were posted. They would, for instance, watch for troop redeployment or changes in training schedules. As one British attaché put it, "Certainly [an agent] must keep his eyes and ears open and miss nothing, but secret service is not his business." It soon became his business.

With European nations spying and counterspying as their countries edged closer to war, President Woodrow Wilson kept the United States on a course of neutrality. He didn't want the nation involved in any activities, including espionage, that might imply that the U.S. was taking sides in the growing tension. In one of the ironies of World War I, the entry of the United States into a war in Europe started in Mexico. President Wilson had long been uneasy about the unstable political situation in Mexico. In 1911 things took a turn for the worse when Porfirio Díaz, Wilson's choice as leader of Mexico, was overthrown by Francisco Madero. Madero was then overthrown by General Victoriano Huerta in 1913. To make matters horribly worse, Huerta ordered the murder of Madero and his vice president.

Outraged by such treachery, Wilson refused to recognize the Huerta government. Things turned against the Huerta regime when two insurgents threatened his leadership: General Venustiano Carranza and Francisco "Pancho" Villa. Despite the fact that Wilson supplied Villa with arms—a questionable move by a president with a noninterventionist policy—Villa and his men were unable to overthrow Huerta.

Because the United States was receiving almost no intelligence from field agents about the situation in Mexico, President Wilson could only wait for events to unfold and then react to them. Faced with a situation that had the potential to sweep across the unprotected two-thousand-mile border between the two countries, Wilson did nothing to authorize an intelligence agency to gather information that could benefit the United States.

To make matters worse, Villa used the arms that the United States had given to him against American citizens. On January 10, 1916, Villa and his small band of rebels stopped a train near Santa Ysabel in Mexico and kidnapped then murdered eighteen young American mining engineers. Two months later, Villa and an army of about five hundred men rode into Columbus, New Mexico, and shot up the town, killing fifteen Americans and wounding many others. Wilson was finally driven to action, ordering Brigadier General John "Black Jack" Pershing and a contingent of U.S. troops over the border into Mexico. But Pershing could not count on having any consistent and reliable intelligence, particularly from local citizens.

Many historians consider 1915 to be the low point of American military intelligence. That was the year that intelligence work came to a halt in the General Staff's War College Division. The timing could not have been worse for the U.S. Not only was the country facing problems with Villa, but Germany was also about to begin making overtures to

Brigadier General John "Black Jack" Pershing

Mexico about playing a part in Germany's plans for victory in the war. Still, the U.S. did nothing to improve intelligence gathering.

"Black Jack" Pershing was not about to wait for the government to debate the issue of intelligence. He moved quickly and resolutely to fill the intelligence void in which he was expected to operate by creating his own spy operation. Cavalry Major James A. Ryan was in charge of the operation for a short time before turning over command to Captain W. O. Reed, who increased the number of operatives to provide intelligence on Pancho Villa. Reed added twenty Apache scouts to his operations.

Japanese-American relations had, meanwhile, been strained for some time over U.S. immigration policies. A 1905 peace treaty brokered by President Theodore Roosevelt had failed to completely satisfy the Japanese, and although the so-called Gentlemen's Agreement of 1907–1908 eased the situation, Roosevelt remained wary.

Roosevelt's misgivings seemed to be validated in 1911 when it was rumored that Japan had sent representatives to discuss the possibility of establishing a base on Magdalena Bay, on Mexico's west coast. There were even signs that a large number of Japanese soldiers had conducted training operations in the Sonoran Desert, to the north of the Gulf of California. It was believed that some of those soldiers had crossed the border into California. But, once again, the United States did not have the intelligence capacity to discover such operations *before* they were carried out.

Faced with the pressing needs for information on these two fronts, then—the hunt for Pancho Villa and threats from the Japanese—as well as a significant German presence in Mexico, Wilson finally (and grudgingly) agreed to allow a spy operation in Mexico. The Office of Naval Intelligence (ONI) hired operatives in Mexico to report on activities involving both Japanese and German representatives. To bolster this meager operation, the ONI also solicited volunteer spies from some of the large U.S. corporations operating in Latin America, including Standard Oil and United Fruit. With so much at stake, these companies were eager to help. Although this effort improved the situation, Pershing and his team never were able to run Villa down.

Germany's covert operations in Mexico had so far been limited to the political arena, mostly connected with propaganda. Berlin secretly subsidized a handful of Mexican newspapers to serve as outlets for propaganda operations. At the same time, Carranza's government was actively courting Germany in the hope of building a closer economic and military relationship with Berlin. The German foreign minister, Arthur Zimmermann, did everything he could to nurture such a relationship with a country bordering the United States, hoping that with the inducement of trade and arms, Carranza would engage the U.S. in conflicts that would require troops and supplies, forcing America to focus its attention and military funding south of the border rather than in Europe.

Getting Mexico into position to engage the United States remained high on the list of German covert operations in the Western Hemisphere. Living in exile, President Huerta was more than willing to draw the U.S. into war. In return Huerta wanted money from the Germans to buy arms and munitions, which he wanted delivered by German submarines. He also wanted reassurance that Berlin would stand behind him if needed.

Sabotage on U.S. Soil

When Huerta was arrested by U.S. agents on June 25, 1915, the Germans decided to change tactics and bring their espionage operations across the border into the U.S. By this time, it was clear to Berlin that the war was not going to be short and swift, as they had expected. Further, if they wanted to win the war, they needed to make certain that the U.S. stayed out of it. They also wanted to put a choke hold on the flood of arms and other war supplies from U.S. ports to England. To reach that goal, Walther Nicolai, cunning German spymaster, created an espionage plan for his operatives in the United States that would make use of political, psychological, economic, and paramilitary strategies.

To begin their campaign of psychological and political dirty tricks, Berlin hired an American public relations man, William Bayard Hale, to serve as their propagandist. In addition to inserting pro-German articles in American city newspapers, Berlin funded *The Fatherland,* a weekly newspaper in the U.S. Berlin also purchased the *Mail and Express,* an established New York City newspaper, as another outlet for their propaganda.

In addition to out-and-out blatant propaganda, the newspapers published features that were aimed at Americans who were not necessarily pro-German but who could be counted on for help. For example, they tried to appeal to the Irish, with their strong anti-British attitude. Germany also tried to attract isolationists and pacifists, who felt the United States should not meddle in the affairs of sovereign European nations. The Germans were hoping to ignite a grassroots movement that would forcefully protest any American involvement in the war, including sending arms or troops.

The German Information Service (GIS) was what is known as a white propaganda agency. Such white groups operated within the limits of the law as they tried to derail any efforts of the U.S. government to enter the war. The GIS published a daily list of pro-German editorials and articles that would attract the attention of resident German aliens as well as German Americans.

The most direct attempt by Germany to curtail the production of war supplies was its creation of the Bridgeport Projectile Company (BPC). In the language of the espionage establishment, BPC was a proprietary company, a front for their efforts to limit munitions that could be sent to the Allies. They ordered huge quantities of materials deemed essential to fight the war. For example, BPC placed orders for machine tools and hydraulic presses, thus making them unavailable for legitimate companies that needed such parts to produce war supplies. BPC also ordered five million pounds of gunpowder from Aetna Powder Company, an order so large that Aetna could sell no powder to the U.S. government.

Merely ordering the parts created a shortage of machine parts that slowed down production of wartime necessities. German agents likewise tried to corner the market on chlorine, a poisonous gas that killed uncountable soldiers in the trenches on both sides. The Bridgeport Projectile Company offered inflated wages, thereby causing unrest among workers at other munitions plants. It gladly paid higher wages as part of its plan to upset manufacture of munitions by the United States. BPC did not necessarily even need to produce munitions that could be shipped to Germany. They only needed to keep war materials out of the hands of U.S. manufacturers. Any materials that were delivered were simply stored at the Bridgeport facility. Some were eventually destroyed.

If Berlin hoped to sustain their enormously successful covert operations for an indefinite period of time, those hopes vanished because of a colossal blunder by one of their own, Dr. Heinrich Albert, a German commercial attaché and finance officer for the German espionage operation in the United States. As finance officer, he was responsible for paying operatives in this country. He chose the wrong time to become forgetful, and U.S. agents were there to take advantage of his error.

William G. McAdoo, secretary of the treasury, authorized a covert operation, assigning Secret Service agents to follow several German and Austro-Hungarian attachés who were under suspicion of espionage. On July 24, 1915, the surveillance team of Special Agents William Houghton and Frank Burke followed George Sylvester Viereck, editor of *The Fatherland*, and Dr. Heinrich Albert, when they left Albert's office in New York. The men boarded a Sixth Avenue elevated train, Houghton and Burke right behind them. Viereck got off the train at Twenty-third Street, with Houghton tailing him.

From his seat right behind the attaché, Agent Burke studied Albert. A heavyset man, measuring about six feet tall, he bore crosscut saber scars on his right cheek. Burke also noted a briefcase beside the German. Albert opened a newspaper and was soon caught up in the news of the day before he nodded off. Startled by the sudden arrival at his station at Fiftieth Street, Albert bolted from his seat and hurried off the train. Burke knew he didn't need to follow Albert any longer when he noticed that Albert had left his briefcase behind. A woman passenger called out to Albert, pointing to his briefcase. But before Albert could reenter the train, Agent Burke snatched the briefcase. As Albert pushed his way back into the car, Burke dashed out the other door of the car, with Albert close behind him. The chase was on until Burke leaped onto a streetcar. He told the conductor that the madman following him had caused a ruckus at the train station. The conductor took one look at Albert, running down the street, wildly waving his arms, and told the motorman not to stop at the next corner. The streetcar moved on, leaving Albert behind.

The briefcase was jammed with telegrams from Berlin, communication for Albert's spies and agents, and financial records. When Secretary McAdoo read the translated documents, he was astounded to learn about the workings of the Bridgeport Projectile Company and the German financing of *The Fatherland*. But he also realized that, as underhanded as the covert actions of the German agents were, he could see no federal law that had been violated. With the prospect of arrest and legal action against these agents improbable, McAdoo was determined to expose the treachery of German agents on U.S. soil in a way that would still put the agents out of business: publicity.

McAdoo handed the documents over to the editor of the *New York World*. The headlines of the next edition screamed the news across page one: "How Germany Has Worked in the U.S. to Shape Opinion, Block the Allies, and Get Munitions for Herself Told in Secret Agent's Letters." Included in the front-page article, which nearly filled the entire page, were documents and a reproduction of two letters. Germany's secrets were revealed for all Americans to read.

Count Johann von Bernstorff, German ambassador to the United States, later called the affair "merely a storm in a teacup," pointing out that there was no evidence to show that any law had been broken. True enough, but, as one historian observed, the publicity not only neutralized the "huge and expensive" covert psychological operation; it was also "made to backfire, dealing a devastating blow" to Germany. And, as Captain Franz von Papen, German military attaché in Mexico City, later admitted, "Our contracts [for war materials] were challenged, cancelled, or replaced by other 'priority' orders, and our scheme came to an end." American munitions manufacturers were no longer wasting time and material filling phony orders for Germany. These supplies could now be used for legitimate U.S. orders.

While the U.S. intelligence community could feel justifiable satisfaction in rolling up the German psychological and propaganda machine, they were not nearly as successful in preventing the sabotage operations carried out by German agents in the United States. German saboteurs targeted many plants, mostly in the northeast, that manufactured arms, munitions, and other supplies for the Allies. That the efforts of German agents were so successful is an indication of how the U.S. counterintelligence community was woefully unprepared.

On November 11, 1914, the German General Staff approved "hiring destructive agents among agents of anarchist organizations." About two weeks later, the German Intelligence Bureau of the High Sea Fleet General Staff put forth a similar order for all "destruction agents" to "mobilize immediately." The General Staff was especially keen on agents in or near commercial operations and military bases "where munitions are being loaded on ships going to England, France, Canada, the United States of North America and Russia."

With orders issued, it wasn't long before American plants and facilities were targeted. On New Year's Day, a destructive fire of suspicious but unknown origin burned out a plant that manufactured wire cable in Trenton, New Jersey. Two days later, an explosion rocked the SS *Orton,* anchored in the Erie Basin in Brooklyn, New York. Other fires and explosions ripped through a number of New Jersey plants that produced weapons or gunpowder. In April a ship carrying arms caught fire at sea. Bombs were found on two others. But the worst was yet to come.

The German consul in San Francisco, Franz von Bopp, ordered that time bombs be hidden on four ships at anchor in Tacoma, Washington. Filled with gunpowder and destined for Russia, the ships were a prime target. The saboteurs did their work well. Explosions rocked Tacoma and nearby Seattle, destroying all the powder. The U.S. still had no counterintelligence system that might have alerted them to such bomb-making operations.

Two of the men who took part in the Tacoma sabotage, Kurt Jahnke and Lothar Witzke, were sent east by von Bopp to work with a sabotage ring that was operating in the New York City–New Jersey area. The men had hoped to plant bombs along the way on trains carrying thousands of horses and mules east for shipment to Europe. An alternative to this plan was to infect the animals with anthrax cultures and an infectious disease called glanders. Fortunately, neither plan was carried out.

The spring and summer of 1915 was a busy time for saboteurs, including Jahnke and Witzke. Eight arms ships caught fire at sea. Bombs were discovered on another five ships. In addition, explosions and fire destroyed arms and powder plants in Wallington, Carney's Point (three times), and Pompton Lakes, New Jersey. The operatives also scored hits at similar plants in Wilmington, Delaware (twice); Philadelphia, Pittsburgh, and Acton, Massachusetts. An arms train was wrecked in New Jersey.

Despite the success of the saboteurs, the German High Command was not satisfied with the work of their spy and sabotage operations. To direct what they hoped would be more destructive results, they sent Captain Franz von Rintelen, a junior member of the admiralty, to New York in 1915. His orders were clear. He was expected to do more to curtail the tons of war supplies, especially munitions, that were bound to Allied soldiers. Such supplies, Berlin believed, were prolonging the war. Von Rintelen felt confident that he would succeed. As he put it, "I'll buy up what I can and blow up what I can't."

Realizing that so much of the war supplies passed through New York Harbor from docks and warehouses in Manhattan and New Jersey, von Rintelen decided that his base of operations should be there. Why travel the country looking for munitions factories to blow up, he reasoned, when his band of operatives could focus on the shipping in New York Harbor and, in a sense, have the munitions come to them?

Von Rintelen promptly converted one of the German merchant ships quarantined in New York Harbor into a bomb factory. He enlisted the help of Dr. Walter T. Scheele, a German chemist, who'd been in the country for a long time (such a person is called a sleeper agent) and Charles Schmidt, the chief engineer of the ship. Together they designed a device that would wreak havoc on munitions ships on the high seas. The bomb-making teacher began by cutting tubing into pieces seven inches or so long, about the size of a large cigar, then dividing the "cigar" into two watertight chambers, separated by a thin copper disk. The cigar bombs were then moved to Dr. Scheele's laboratory in Hoboken, New Jersey, where he filled one chamber with sulfuric acid, the other with the highly explosive picric acid. The copper disk that separated the two acids needed to withstand the caustic effects of the acid for a sufficient period of time to allow the ship on which it was hidden to move out of the harbor and begin steaming toward England.

When a ship carrying Dr. Scheele's "cigars" was on the high seas, the copper disk would corrode, allowing the acid in both chambers to mix, igniting a fire that was intense enough to melt the wax plugs on each end of the cigar. When the wax plugs melted, the fire received more oxygen, allowing it to burn more fiercely. Left undetected in a ship's cargo hold, the fire would quickly spread, often destroying the cargo and even the ship itself. Before too long, the bomb factory was producing as many as fifty "cigars" each day. Von Rintelen set up similar bomb factories in the U.S. port cities of Boston, Philadelphia, Baltimore, and New Orleans.

Von Rintelen's first success was aboard the SS *Phoebus,* which was hauling artillery shells to Russia. The cigars did their work, causing a fire that was discovered before it had destroyed all the shells. However, to put out the flames, the captain flooded the hold, turning the shells into useless hunks of metal. About half the ships with the hidden fire-bombs, sometimes as many as thirty "cigars," made it safely to port, more than likely because the bombs failed to ignite. Nonetheless, the string of mysterious cargo fires aboard U.S. ships continued through the spring.

With the success of von Rintelen's sabotage operations at a new high—the U.S. government had been unable to detect or infiltrate the spy rings—he was ready for a bigger challenge, and it didn't take him long to find it. He would go after the Lehigh Valley Railroad Company's huge terminal located on Black Tom Island, a point of land that juts out from Jersey City, New Jersey, across New York Harbor's Upper Bay from Brooklyn, New York. The huge terminal was located at the southern end of what is today called Liberty State Park. It was, in fact, the busiest wartime port on the East Coast. Because federal law allowed munitions to be stored on Black Tom for only twenty-four hours, it was very busy. Ships of all sorts—tugs, barges, freighters—came and went all day.

Inside the terminal, trains were in constant motion as they delivered war supplies—mostly munitions—then reversed direction to be refilled.

According to reports in the *New York Times,* there was plenty of fire power at the terminal on July 30: "11 [railroad] cars of high explosives, 17 of shells, 3 of nitro-allulos, 1 of TNT, and 2 of combination fuses; in all a total of 2,132,000 pounds of explosives." In addition, "ten barges were tied up, most of them loaded with explosives," which they'd taken on at other terminals and piers around New York Harbor.

The chain reaction of disaster began with a fire. One of the private detectives hired to guard the terminal remembered it this way: "The fire had started in the center of the string of cars on shore near the land end of the pier. The flames had gotten too good a start for us to do anything." Of course, the shells soon began to "cook," and shrapnel shells of smaller caliber began to explode. An investigation of the explosions found that an incendiary device—perhaps something like Dr. Scheele's cigar bombs—had been hidden among the boxcars and probably on at least one of the munitions barges. Evidence indicated that the saboteurs had been paying off some of the terminal guards for intelligence about work schedules. Some investigators felt that the guards under suspicion likely looked the other way when the German agents arrived that night to do their damage.

Aftermath of the attack on Black Tom Island

The blasts were spectacular, rocking communities in New Jersey and New York. In fact, the tremor of the blast was felt as far away as Philadelphia, one hundred miles south. Windows shattered twenty-five miles from the blast. In Jersey City, a hunk of shrapnel rocketed into the clock tower of the *Jersey Journal* building, stopping the clock at exactly 2:13. The Statue of Liberty, on Bedloe's Island, was only about 650 yards from Black Tom. The force of the explosion popped about a hundred of Lady Liberty's rivets and her copper skin was pelted with shrapnel. (After inspection of the monument, no tourists were allowed in the torch.) The explosion also damaged Ellis Island, about a mile from the blast site. The high vaulted ceiling of the main hall collapsed, nearly every window shattered, and sections of the roof were damaged. All the while, of course, the sky was filled with a dangerous shower of shrapnel, shells, and burning debris.

A damaged pier on Black Tom Island with the Statue of Liberty visible in the distance.

Remarkably, when the fires were extinguished and people were accounted for, there were but seven fatalities in the explosions and inferno. This relatively low number of deaths is remarkable considering that almost five hundred people were aboard the ships tied up at the piers and anchored nearby. Scientists believe that the blast was about a 5.0 on the Richter scale. In comparison, the collapse of the World Trade Center north tower on September 11, 2001, registered a 2.3, according to a seismic observatory in New Jersey.

Initially investigations determined that the explosion and fire at Black Tom had been an accident exacerbated by carelessness of the owner of the facility. But further inquiry into the cause of the events of that July 30 led to two experienced saboteurs, Kurt Jahnke and Lothar Witzke. They had apparently teamed up with Michael Kristoff, described as a "mentally deficient Hungarian immigrant," who lived and worked in the area. Jahnke and Witzke eased a small boat alongside one of the piers, where they met Kristoff and carried out their sabotage.

Although the catastrophe at Black Tom Island was by far the largest act of sabotage on American soil to that point, it was, according to the *New York Times*, one of fifty such acts of sabotage in the United States in the first two years of the war, from 1914 until the summer of 1916. Over half of the attacks (twenty-eight of fifty) took place in the New York–New Jersey area.

Mata Hari

AFTER BENEDICT ARNOLD, there is probably no other name that people associate with spying more than that of Mata Hari. But, while Arnold's reputation for spying and treachery is based on facts, Mata Hari's seems to be more fiction than fact. Did she spy for France and Germany in World War I? She did. But her spying was minor in nature, rather than anything resembling the legendary feats and betrayal that are attributed to her.

The Dutch-born Margaretha Zelle began her career as an exotic dancer in Paris; her stage name, Mata Hari, derived from a Malay word meaning "sun" or "dawn." For seven years she was a resounding success in many of the capitals of Europe, which gave her the opportunity to meet men of power. As she approached the age of forty, and the end of her dancing career, she developed "intricate, affectionate, and sometimes exclusive relationships, with men who supported her in elegant style." Many of these men were involved in the highest levels of government and would readily share state or military secrets with her as a boastful sign of their importance.

Some historians believe that she met the German intelligence chief Walther Nicolai in 1916. The meeting was not an accidental encounter. Baron von Mirbach, an intelligence officer in Kleve, in western Germany, remembered seeing Mata Hari dance and felt she would make a good spy. Mirbach believed that German intelligence could take advantage of Mata Hari's popularity with men who had access to information that might help the German war effort.

Nicolai flattered her and put her up in a fancy Hamburg hotel, and she began her spy training. She was schooled on how to make meaningful observations, write reports in invisible ink, and send them to an address in Antwerp.

As it turned out, however, she wrote only a few letters, and they offered no significant intelligence, nothing more than rumors and bits of information that were generally well known. German intelligence decided that this amateur spy was a bigger liability than an asset and that she therefore had to be eliminated. But rather than do the deed

The spy Mata Hari in her days as an exotic dancer

themselves, they planned to maneuver the French into doing it for them.

To this end, they sent coded information about her to their agents in France, referring to her as agent H21, knowing that the code had already been broken by the French. The coded messages were, indeed, intercepted and read by French intelligence officers, sowing the seeds of doubt about Mata Hari in their minds. Was she a double agent working for France and Germany? Or had she simply turned and become a German agent?

Mata Hari returned to Paris to meet with Captain Georges Ladoux, chief of French military intelligence, and on February 13, 1917, Mata Hari was arrested and jailed in Saint Lazare prison, where her treatment was deplorable. She was forced to live in filthy conditions, isolated from other prisoners. She was not permitted to bathe, nor was she provided with a change of clothes. Prison officials allowed her fifteen minutes of physical exercise each day. Despite such horrible circumstances, Mata Hari maintained her innocence during her interrogation sessions, at one point writing a note to the investigator of her case, Pierre Bouchardon, that read, "You have made me suffer too much. I am completely mad. I beg you to put an end to this."

At her trial, it was no surprise to anyone when she was unanimously condemned to death. As a final insult, she was first required to pay court costs. The firing squad assembled in the predawn hours of October 15, 1917.

In the final minutes of her life, Mata Hari faced the thirteen soldiers in the firing squad, her head held high. She refused the customary blindfold. Part of her legend includes the notion that she blew a kiss to the soldiers before shots cracked the morning stillness. Although it was clearly unnecessary, the officer drew his revolver and delivered the traditional coup de grâce, a single shot into the spy's ear. With no one to claim the body, her remains were delivered to a medical school, for dissection by students.

Was Mata Hari a spy? Yes, but a far cry from being the "greatest woman spy" in history. It's debatable if she was, in fact, a double agent. Some historians believe she spent fifteen weeks in a "spy academy," learning the skills of the trade, including using various methods of coded communication, memorizing photographs and maps, and becoming familiar with weapons. Such training would have also included warnings about "fool spies," or double agents. Mata Hari consistently told her interrogators that she never attended any such spy training sessions. Several biographers agree.

Even long after the war, the "little mysteries of counterespionage" prevented all the facts of Mata Hari's case from being released. In fact, when Pierre Bouchardon published his memoir in 1953, he claimed that "professional secrecy" prevented him from saying more about the evidence that convinced him that Mata Hari was a spy who had to face a firing squad.

The Zimmermann Telegram

While U.S. intelligence agencies were not prepared to keep track of and stop German operatives who had slipped into this country, their counterparts in England did have the personnel and system to take on the German espionage machine. True, the British had more at stake in the war, but they also were much better prepared to fight Germany in espionage battles, with some of their best work done in the area of codes and ciphers.

Cable messages from Europe to the United States traveled through transatlantic cables that passed deep in the English Channel. The British saw the cables as an opportunity to gain access to secret diplomatic messages sent from Berlin to its ambassador in Washington, D.C. Knowing they couldn't tap the cables the way they could tap phone lines, the British did the next best thing. The cable ship *Telconia* cut all five of the cables that carried communications through the channel. To make sure that the sabotage had a lasting effect, the *Telconia* rolled up a few of the cable ends on her drums and carried them to England. This act of sabotage was Great Britain's first offensive act of the war.

As a result of the cut cables, Germany lost its most secure long-distance communications system. The Germans now had to rely on radio transmissions from their powerful wireless station at Nauen, a few miles from Berlin. Which was exactly what the British military knew they would have to do. And once the Germans began sending wireless messages, MI8, the British code breakers, began plucking them from the air. Of course, all German correspondence was sent in a complicated cipher system, so that was when the hard work began for the code breakers of MI8.

The intercepted messages were usually no more than rows of numbers in four- and five-digit groups, with an occasional three-number group included. For example, *67893* was the code word for *Mexico*. Such messages, sometimes as many as two hundred a day, were snagged day and night by the operators in Room 40, MI8's cryptography center. To make the messages more difficult to decipher, the Germans frequently added another layer of security to their text by enciphering a message that was already written in code! In other words, the British code breakers needed to solve the cipher message before they could even take a crack at the coded message.

Given how this double disguising of a secret message could make decoding so much more difficult, it remains a mystery why the German telegram that finally convinced the American president to join the Allies on the battlefield in 1917 was simply a coded message.

While the task that faced the cryptanalysts in Room 40 was very intellectually demanding and physically taxing, the Germans committed some blunders in the way they sent their secret radio messages, giving the British help in their task. The first mistake of German intelligence was the error of arrogance, believing that the British were not up to the challenge of deciphering their messages. Another mistake they made was sending duplicates and even triplicates of some of their messages, with each one using a different cipher key. This ill-advised practice meant that the code breakers had a couple of different versions of the same message, giving them a much better chance of cracking the cipher. The men of Room 40 were, in the words of one historian, "reading Berlin's messages more quickly and correctly than the German recipients." This group of cryptography amateurs, who were generally recruited from college faculties, was able to achieve its success with "ingenuity, endless patience, and sparks of inspired guessing."

On several occasions Room 40 received an unexpected but welcome gift when a German codebook was recovered after a sea battle and presented to the British code breakers. One such gift was a codebook from the German ship *Magdeburg*, a light cruiser that ran aground on an island off of Finland. When Russian ships quickly bore down on the cruiser, the captain of the stranded ship immediately did what all naval officers were taught to do: he ordered his signalman to bring him the ship's codebook so he could throw the book, wrapped in lead covers, into the sea. But before the signalman could deliver the book to his captain, he was killed by Russian guns. When the Russians recovered his body, the sailor was still clutching the codebook in his arms.

The Russian admiralty decided that their British allies could make better use of the codebook than they could, so it was sent to London. The codebook was a bonanza for the British code breakers. Not only did it contain the columns of code "words"—groups of randomly selected numbers— on which the messages were based, but it also included a changeable key to the cipher systems used to obscure the coded messages.

The director of Room 40, Admiral Sir William Reginald Hall, was constantly on the lookout for any German codebook he could get his hands on. In December an iron-encased sea chest was delivered to his office. The chest had been hauled to the surface in the net of a British fishing trawler. It turned out that the chest was from a German destroyer that had been cornered and sunk by British warships. Among the personal papers and nautical charts in the chest, Hall discovered a codebook. It took the code breakers of Room 40 a few months to discover that the book contained the code system used by the German military to communicate with their naval atta- chés abroad.

After hours of hard work and their "inspired guess- ing," the code breakers scored many triumphs. Their greatest success, however, came in 1917, when the war was at a critical point.

For nearly three years the war had taken its toll on the fighting nations. England maintained hope that, despite President Woodrow Wilson's continued belief in his brand of neutrality, the Americans would reconsider, join the fight, and tip the balance of war in favor of the Allies.

On January 16, 1917, in a clear attempt to convince the Mexican government to help Germany in the war, Arthur Zimmermann, the German foreign secretary, sent a telegram to Count von Bernstorff, the German ambassador in Washington. The foreign secretary wanted to be certain that this message reached von Bernstorff, so he made arrangements for it to be carried aboard a U-boat to Sweden and from there to Washington through diplomatic channels.

As luck would have it, the departure of the sub was delayed. Impatient, Zimmermann turned to his second option: sending the message to his ambassador through the U.S. State Department. Although Wilson considered the United States to be neutral, he allowed messages to be sent to von Bernstorff via the State Department as a courtesy. The telegram sent, Zimmermann waited for a reply. What Zimmermann didn't know was that the British were doing a thorough job of intercepting German wireless transmissions.

The first thing about the Zimmermann telegram that two Room 40 code breakers, Reverend William Montgomery and

Nigel de Grey, noticed was its length, more than a thousand groups. Although the length itself was not suspicious, it *was* out of the ordinary. Then de Grey noticed the top group of numbers in the message, *13042,* a variation of *13040,* indicated a German diplomatic code. Since Room 40 had a copy of the *13040* codebook, they began using it to decipher the message.

As Montgomery and de Grey slowly made their way through the message, they noticed more and more oddities. For example, *97556* appeared near the end of the message; the *90000* family indicated important names that were not used very often in messages. We can imagine their shock when they realized that *97556* stood for *Zimmermann.* That single name fired the men with excitement as they began working on the message from the beginning.

In time, some of the coded "words" began to give up their secrets. They found *most secret* and *For Your Excellency's personal information.* The men pushed on, discovering *Mexico* and *Japan* in the text. What could that mean? And what was Germany's interest in Mexico? How did Japan figure into the plan? The men could not think of a reason for the connection among Germany, Japan, and Mexico. Quickly thumbing the pages of the codebook, the men worked on at a fever pitch.

They learned that there were two parts to the telegram. The first part—the longer of the two—carried bad

WESTERN UNION
TELEGRAM

NEWCOMB CARLTON, PRESIDENT

CLASS OF SERVICE DESIRED
Fast Day Message
Day Letter
Night Message
Night Letter

Patrons should mark an X oppo-
site the class of service desired;
OTHERWISE THE TELEGRAM
WILL BE TRANSMITTED AS A
FAST DAY MESSAGE.

Send the following telegram, subject to the terms
on back hereof, which are hereby agreed to

via Galveston

JAN 19 1917

GERMAN LEGATION

MEXICO CITY

130	13042	13401	8501	115	3528	416	17214	6491	11310
18147	18222	21560	10247	11518	23677	13605	3494	14936	
98092	5905	11311	10392	10371	0302	21290	5161	39695	
23571	17504	11269	18276	18101	0317	0228	17694	4473	
23284	22200	19452	21589	67893	5569	13918	8958	12137	
1333	4725	4458	5905	17166	13851	4458	17149	14471	6706
13850	12224	6929	14991	7382	15857	67893	14218	36477	
5870	17553	67893	5870	5454	16102	15217	22801	17138	
21001	17388	7446	23638	18222	6719	14331	15021	23845	
3156	23552	22096	21604	4797	9497	22464	20855	4377	
23610	18140	22260	5905	13347	20420	39689	13732	20667	
6929	5275	18507	52262	1340	22049	13339	11265	22295	
10439	14814	4178	6992	8784	7632	7357	6926	52262	11267
21100	21272	9346	9559	22464	15874	18502	18500	15857	
2188	5376	7381	98092	16127	13486	9350	9220	76036	14219
5144	2831	17920	11347	17142	11264	7667	7762	15099	9110
10482	97556	3569	3670						

BERNSTOPFF.

Charge German Embassy.

The Zimmermann Telegram

news for all ships at sea, but especially American ones. Zimmermann was informing von Bernstorff that the German U-boat fleet would resume "unrestricted" submarine warfare on February 1. From that day onward, all ships, even those from neutral nations, would be fair game for deadly submarines patrolling the dark waters of the Atlantic.

Indeed, on February 3, the American steamship *Housatonic* was torpedoed without warning. This unprovoked attack on a passenger ship was another in a long line of similar acts of belligerence that had occurred in previous years. The most famous was the sinking of the steamship *Lusitania* in 1915, which killed all but two dozen of its 1,924 passengers, 114 of whom were Americans. The United States demanded that Germany disavow the attack on the *Lusitania* and make immediate restitution. Germany refused to do either. In March 1916 the French *Sussex* was sunk by a German submarine attack in the English Channel. The United States threatened to cut off diplomatic relations with Germany unless such attacks stopped.

If the first part of the telegram was ominous, the second section must have sent shivers of fear through Montgomery and de Grey. Although there were about thirty spots in the message that the men could not figure out, they had learned enough to know that it was time for them to notify their superior of their discovery.

Montgomery quickly fetched Admiral Hall. The head of Room 40, nicknamed "Blinker" for the uncontrollable twitching in his eyes, hurried into the room and stood in front of de Grey's desk. Without saying a word, de Grey stood and handed the message to the small, ruddy-faced man. Hall's eyes took in what Montgomery and de Grey had discovered. His eye twitches became more pronounced as he tried to assess the impact of what he was reading.

Hall well understood the gamble the Germans were taking. In two weeks they would unleash the full fury of their two hundred U-boats, in an effort to choke off the stream of American supplies that was keeping the Allied nations in the war. Surely, the U.S. would not permit their ships to be sunk by a belligerent nation. They would retaliate—unless their forces and attention were focused on a hot spot closer to home. Germany wanted Mexico to engage the Americans enough so they would be unable to send troops to help the Allies.

Zimmermann did not spell out what he hoped Mexico could do to assist the German war effort. The Germans weren't looking for a long-term commitment, confident, as the telegram states, that the submarine warfare would compel "England to make peace within a few months." With Mexico sharing an extensive border with the United States, perhaps Germany expected Mexico to stage attacks in their "lost territories in Texas, New Mexico, and Arizona."

Arthur Zimmermann had no idea that "Blinker" Hall had read his secret message. But now that Hall had read it, what could he do with this information? On one hand, he believed that President Wilson, faced with the information in the telegram, would declare war on Germany. On the other hand, to share the telegram with Wilson would surely alert Berlin that the British had been reading their secret messages. As he walked back to his office, Hall considered ways that he could share the intelligence in the Zimmermann telegram and establish its authenticity without letting Berlin know that Room 40 had intercepted and read hundreds of their secret messages.

Hall decided that he needed to find a way to get a copy of the telegram that von Bernstorff would next have sent to Heinrich von Eckardt, the German ambassador in Mexico. He was convinced that there would be small but helpful differences between the original telegram sent by Zimmermann and the version that von Bernstorff would have sent to Mexico City. The message itself would be the same. Hall was sure that von Bernstorff would copy it carefully, but he was equally certain that it would contain telltale differences. For one thing, the dateline at the top of the telegram would be different, as well as the address and the signature. Yes, he needed to get his hands on a copy of *that* telegram, which would provide Wilson and Congress with proof of Germany's intent with Mexico without compromising the activities of Room 40. Hall counted on Berlin to blame someone at the embassy or in the Mexico City telegraph office for letting the telegram fall into the hands of the Americans.

But how would Hall get that telegram? That would take some doing, he admitted. Then Hall remembered Mr. H., one of his trusted operatives. It was Mr. H. who had alerted MI8 to the suspicious activities of Sweden's chargé d'affaires in Mexico City, Folke Cronholm. Sharp-eyed Mr. H. had noticed that Cronholm was making frequent visits to the telegraph office, far more visits than one would expect from a representative of the Swedish government, given the limited relationship between that government and Mexico.

Mr. H.'s report on Cronholm included a mention of the fact that von Eckardt had recommended Cronholm for an official decoration because, as the German ambassador wrote, Cronholm "arranges the conditions for the official telegraphic traffic for your Excellency." Odd, Hall had thought on reading this, that Berlin would not simply give Cronholm some second-tier medal in a private ceremony. Why such public recognition for the Swedish diplomat?

Hall could think of only one reason for such an honor. And that reason stunned him. Was Cronholm helping to transmit coded German messages overseas? The answer came as soon as Room 40 deciphered some intercepted

Swedish cable messages. As expected, each one began with a handful of Swedish code groups. However, the messages continued in German. Room 40 took to calling this ruse the Swedish Roundhouse. With this new information, British intelligence had begun monitoring Swedish cables. And it had all started with the keen observations of Mr. H. Now Hall wondered if Mr. H. could assist him again. He contacted his operative and made his request. Then he waited for Mr. H. to do his work.

Mr. H. quickly began talking to his contacts in the city. Soon he heard of a British printer in Mexico City who had been falsely arrested for printing counterfeit money. Mr. H. intervened with the British minister, who got the frightened printer released from custody and the charges against him dropped. The printer, overjoyed to be free, told Mr. H. that he would welcome the opportunity to repay the agent for his intervention. As a matter of fact, Mr. H. told him, there *was* a favor the printer could do for him.

The British agent had learned that the printer's good friend—in fact, the first person he contacted for advice when the accusation leveled at him sent him into a panic—worked in the Mexican Telegraphic Office. Would he be able, Mr. H. wondered, to get a copy of the original telegram sent by von Bernstorff to von Eckardt? The printer was sure his friend could do that. He was as good as his word.

Once Hall received the telegram from his agent, he was ready to approach President Wilson.

British government leaders didn't present the Zimmermann telegram to Wilson for a few weeks. Hall reminded them that outrage was growing in America over Germany's announcement late in the day of January 31 that the German navy would resume unrestricted submarine warfare. In fact, that policy provoked the U.S. government to cut diplomatic relations with Germany in February.

On February 24, when Hall sensed that the Zimmermann telegram would tip the balance in favor of the U.S. joining the Allied forces, the British home secretary presented the telegram to President Wilson. One week later, news of the Zimmermann telegram was splashed across the front page of American newspapers. On April 6, 1917, the Congress of the United States declared war on Germany and its allies.

Although the battlefield mayhem continued for another year, the added strength of U.S. troops proved to be too much for Germany. David Kahn, a leading authority of cryptography, wrote this about the Zimmermann telegram: "Never before or since has so much turned upon the solution of a secret message."

By the time the war ended, the United States military recognized that it could no longer rely on other nations to provide it with crucial intelligence. Nor could it continue with the limited intelligence operations that it had established. Although World War II was more than twenty years in the future, the U.S. military was set on a course of developing a comprehensive intelligence network.

Choctaw Code Talkers

WHILE MATA HARI'S DRAMA played out in France, soldiers of the American Expeditionary Force were thrust into the thick of the horrible trench war in the same country. Braving mustard gas that burned their lungs and relentless machine-gun fire, the Allied forces held their ground. Nonetheless, things were looking grim for the Americans in the Meuse-Argonne campaign when they found themselves surrounded by the German army, making its last offensive push of the war.

When the Americans tried to send a message to headquarters pleading for help or discussing strategy, they suspected that the phone lines were tapped by the Germans. To verify their misgivings about the phone lines, they "let slip" a rumor that they were moving their supply depot. Part of this disinformation was the map coordinates that indicated where the supply depot would be. Within thirty minutes, the area that matched those coordinates came under heavy bombardment from German artillery. Even though the Americans encoded their messages, the German code breakers were able to easily crack the code and act on the intelligence that they discovered, making the American position even more dire.

The Germans seemed to have mastered many of the essentials of spy craft, and the Americans still did not have the counterintelligence apparatus to match them. Then, one night in early October, an army captain accidentally discovered a way to foil the German's ability to break their codes. On that evening, Captain Lawrence was taking his customary walk among his men of the 36th Division of the 142nd Infantry Regiment when he overheard a conversation between two of them in a language he'd never heard before.

Curious, he asked the men what language they were speaking. One of them, Corporal Solomon Lewis, told Lawrence that they were speaking in Choctaw, their tribal language. Lawrence stared at the men, an idea growing in his mind. He asked if there were any other Choctaw speakers in the battalion. Lewis and his friend, Private Mitchell Bobb, figured there were eight others. In fact, two of them, Ben Caterby and Pete Maytubby, worked at headquarters.

With Lewis and Bobb at his side, Lawrence hurried to the communications tent. He called headquarters and told his commander to get Caterby and Maytubby, then stand by for a message. Lawrence's idea was simple. He would dictate a message to Lewis and Bobb, who would translate it into Choctaw, then use a field phone to relay the message to Caterby and Maytubby, who would translate the message for their commander.

They quickly discovered, however, that there was one obstacle to overcome before the Choctaw could communicate essential military information: the language had no words for modern military terms, such as *artillery, machine gun,* or

A group of Choctaw code talkers

battalion. So Lewis, Bobb, and Lawrence put their heads together and came up with Choctaw words that could stand for such terms, including *big gun* for *artillery, little gun shoot fast* for *machine gun,* and ears of corn to indicate numbers of battalions. Filled with excitement, Lewis and Bobb made history that night in 1917 when they transmitted the first military message in the Choctaw language.

The plan was such a success that the commander ordered one Choctaw code talker be assigned to each field company headquarters. The first official use of the Choctaw code talkers gave the orders for two of the companies to withdraw from Chardeny on the night of October 26, 1917. The retreat was a success, and the use of messages transmitted in Choctaw grew. On October 27, the men used the code to plan an attack at Forest Ferme that came as a complete surprise to the Germans.

One can imagine the shock of the German code breakers when they started hearing the Choctaw messages. Remember, by so easily cracking a code system used previously by the Americans, the Germans had enjoyed complete access to intelligence sent by the American army. Suddenly, that changed. They were faced with a code that they couldn't break because it was not based on a European language or the mathematical progressions that code breakers rely on. In fact, one captured German officer later said that their intelligence gatherers "were completely confused by the Indian language and gained no benefit whatsoever from their wiretaps."

Within seventy-two hours of the initial Choctaw transmissions, the tide of battle turned. The American and Allied troops took the offensive, driving the Germans into full retreat. Because the war ended very shortly after Meuse-Argonne, the Choctaw code talkers didn't get another opportunity to use their code in battle. But Choctaw and other Native Americans, mostly Navajos, served in a similar capacity in World War II.

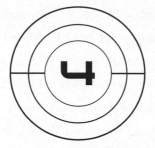

Espionage Gets Organized in World War II

On September 1, 1939, the Nazis invaded Poland, setting in motion a chain of events that would lead to World War II. Although the United States was not involved in the war in its first years, President Franklin D. Roosevelt was, of course, deeply concerned with what was happening in Europe. He well understood that the U.S. had remained on the sidelines before they were drawn into fighting World War I. He knew that intelligence operations in the United States were still confined to sections within the army and navy, and he wasn't convinced the nation's intelligence operations were as good as they should be.

Wanting to get a better understanding of the war in Europe, the president sent his old friend William Donovan to England to observe how the British were prepared for war. Donovan was a World War I hero and commander of the legendary Fighting 69th, a regiment founded by Irish immigrants. Donovan, wounded three times in the war, was awarded the Congressional Medal of Honor and remains one of the most decorated soldiers in American history. Since the war, "Wild Bill" Donovan, as he was called since his army days, had become a partner at a successful Wall Street firm and had many well-connected friends serving as bankers, corporate lawyers, economists, university professors, and adventurers.

While in England, Donovan met with members of the Secret Intelligence Service (SIS), known as MI6 (Military Intelligence Section 6), to assess the work of the British overseas espionage organization. Sir William Stephenson, the chief of SIS operations in the Western Hemisphere, convinced Donovan that the United States needed an agency like the Special Operations Executive (SOE), the U.K.'s central intelligence agency.

When Donovan returned to the U.S., he presented Roosevelt with his report that made a strong case for a centralized intelligence agency. The president was won over by Donovan's argument and on July 11, 1941, signed a directive establishing the position of Coordinator of Information

(COI). The person in this position would be authorized to "collect and analyze all information and data, which may bear upon national security; to correlate such information and data, and to make such information and data available to the President . . . and to carry out, when requested by the President, such supplementary activities as may facilitate the securing of information important for national security not now available to the Government." William Donovan was chosen to fill this new position.

Donovan had been in his new position for only about five months when the Japanese attacked Pearl Harbor, on December 7, 1941. This "date which will live in infamy," in the words of Roosevelt, was the day the United States was thrust into World War II. Americans were stunned by the audacious surprise attack. Politicians and military men wondered how such an intelligence failure was possible. With the United States at war, the COI and military intelligence were forced to work together more than they had in the past and more than they cared to.

About six months after Pearl Harbor, the office of the COI was renamed the Office of Strategic Services (OSS). The OSS became what many military historians consider America's first central intelligence agency. And Bill Donovan began his work to coordinate a number of clandestine activities that supported the war effort, including intelligence gathering and reporting, creating propaganda, spreading misinformation, sabotage, subversion behind enemy lines, and a number of other related activities.

There are always rivalries and turf battles in any large organization, and the intelligence community is no exception. OSS and the intelligence branches of the army and navy worked together only when they had to. (Some historians believe that a lack of communication among the military intelligence agencies allowed the Japanese clear sailing to Pearl Harbor.) In England the SOE had a similar relationship with MI6. Part of the reason for such poor working relationships was a matter of style. The OSS and SOE were more spontaneous, less "by the book," which did not sit well with military and intelligence establishments. For the most part, however, the OSS and SOE worked well together in their European operations.

One principle of espionage that both agencies understood is that a spy is often only as successful as the team that supports him or her. This support begins with the agent's training, continues when he or she is in the field, and ends only when the agent returns safely. The OSS and SOE made sure that only young men and women who were able to survive a grueling and intense training were permitted to operate in the field. And they *were* young, especially the women, many of whom were in their early twenties when they began training.

When the agents' training was complete, they were still not ready to go behind enemy lines and put what they had learned to the test. Before they completed their training, they needed to have the tools of the trade, beginning with false identity papers. For instance, the French Document Section prepared whatever papers the agents being sent to France needed, including passports, identification cards, and ration cards. Once an agent was established safely in France, he or she would receive genuine documents from the proper authorities. But until then, the fake papers needed to stand up to close scrutiny. Technicians in the Research and Development Section examined all aspects of French documentation, including ink, paper, glue, and bindings. They understood that the slightest error could mean death for an agent behind enemy lines.

The most important part of a document was the paper it was printed on. Nothing would give away an agent faster than a document with crisp new paper or a paper of better quality than the paper used in France. To overcome this obstacle, the paper needed to be artificially aged. One trick for giving paper a used look was to spread it on the floor and let people repeatedly walk over it. In some cases, paper was rubbed with ash to make it look older than it really was. Agents also needed correct currency to use behind enemy lines, in particular francs and Reichsmarks. The agencies placed a premium on worn coins and bills, which were unlikely to attract attention.

Virginia Hall

A female spy who followed in the footsteps of her sisters who served before her, particularly in the Civil War, was Virginia Hall. Code-named Diane, Hall was one of the most successful woman spies in the history of espionage. By the time her service was complete, "the limping lady," as she was called, was one of the spies most wanted by the Gestapo. As one Gestapo officer put it, "The woman who limps is one of the most dangerous Allied agents in France. We must find her and destroy her."

Although Virginia Hall began college in the U.S., she traveled to Europe to further her language studies, mastering French, German, and Italian. She returned home in 1929 to study French in more depth. She then entered the diplomatic service, working for the U.S. State Department in Poland, Austria, and Turkey. While on a hunting trip in Turkey, she accidentally shot herself in the foot. When gangrene set in, there was nothing doctors could do but amputate her leg below the knee. She was fitted with a wooden leg, which she nicknamed Cuthbert.

Although her wooden leg kept her from working for the State Department as she had wanted — at the time they had a policy of not hiring amputees — Hall wasn't one to let something like an artificial leg stop her from making a contribution.

Alarmed at the growing threat of Nazi Germany throughout Europe, she returned to Europe as a volunteer with the French Ambulance Service Unit. However, when France fell to the Nazis in June 1940, Hall was no longer safe in France. She moved to England and worked as a code clerk at the United States embassy. It didn't take long for the British intelligence community to learn of her work, and she was recruited by the Special Operations Executive.

For her first assignment as a trained SOE agent, Virginia Hall was sent to France at the end of the summer of 1941 to organize resistance fighters and collect intelligence. Her

Assorted fake travel documents used by Virginia Hall

"legend," or fake background story, had been carefully crafted to take advantage of her position as a credentialed journalist for the *New York Post*. Hall would cable her stories to the U.S. with secret intelligence encoded and embedded in them.

While others may have worried that Hall's limp would make her too recognizable to be effective in the field, she learned to compensate by wearing long coats and walking with long strides. She was also a great actor—a master at taking on cover characters.

It was Hall who suggested that agents be sent into Germany posing as French workers, making it less likely that they would come under close scrutiny as they gathered intelligence. She also realized that French cities, whose residents tended to be more sympathetic to the German occupation, were becoming dangerous places for SOE agents. She suggested concentrating agents in rural areas, where people were more sympathetic to the resistance, especially the farmers, who resented being paid so little by the Nazis for their crops. She began organizing resistance fighters in the Lyons area of southern France. Downed airmen or escaped prisoners of war knew that if they got to Lyons, Hall and her contacts would help them to return safely to England.

Virginia Hall had a knack for finding helpful and reliable contacts in Lyons who were ready to provide information or take action. Among them were: Germaine, whose "main interest was helping prisoners"; Pepin, "useful as a postbox" and for arranging a "clinic, ambulance service, doctors, nurses, anaesthetists, etc., for our men"; Eugène, whose girlfriend had a sister and brother-in-law who were "ready to do anything for us"; and Madam Landry, who was "able to get all sorts of fake papers for people." And these are only a handful of French citizens in Lyons and other towns and villages who responded to Virginia Hall and risked their lives to help defeat Hitler.

The situation in France became too dangerous for Virginia Hall early in November 1942. She was alerted to the approaching Allied invasion of North Africa, which would more than likely force German troops to race to the southern part of France. The following day, one of her contacts warned her that the invasion had begun and the Nazis were expected to swarm into Lyons sometime after midnight. Virginia Hall was taking no chances. She packed her bag and started her long journey to London. That night she caught the 11:00 p.m. train to Perpignan, on the Spanish border. Her instincts to flee were on target. The head of the Lyons Gestapo said that he "would give anything to put his hands on that . . . bitch." He never got that chance. When she reached Perpignan, at the foothills of the Pyrenees, a guide was waiting to lead her safely to Barcelona. She arrived in London in January 1943.

While the rushed journey over the Pyrenees would tax even the hardiest of hikers, Virginia Hall made it with a wooden leg that was vexing her for a good part of the journey.

The message she sent London became an enduring legend: "Cuthbert is giving me trouble, but I can cope." The reply, no doubt from a radio operator who knew nothing of Virginia Hall, was curt: "If Cuthbert is giving you trouble, have him eliminated." As one of her French agents said, "God knows how she made the journey over the mountains." Indeed.

After some weeks in England, Hall was ready for her next assignment. This time she was sent to Spain to help organize a version of the Underground Railroad, like the one that existed in the United States during the Civil War. This underground railroad aided escaped prisoners of war, stranded agents, and airmen making their way to London via neutral Spain. She spent much of her time sending messages via wireless, organizing safe houses, and keeping alert for new resistance recruits. But she soon grew restless. She craved the excitement she had experienced in France.

When she expressed her desire to return to France, her SOE superior tried to convince her to go to London as a "briefing officer for the boys." She resisted, and he finally agreed to transfer her to France. Thus, on the evening of March 21, 1944, Virginia Hall arrived by boat on the Brittany coast. After a brief stop in Paris, she set off for the town of Maidons. There she met an old farmer who found her a one-room house, without water or electricity, and invited her to take meals with his wife and him. Since Hall had spent summers on her family's farm, she was familiar with farm chores and offered to repay the farmer for his help by tending his cows. After morning milking, she walked the cows to pasture, always on the lookout for fields that could serve as parachute drop spots or landing strips for small planes. And, as usual, she was always studying the people, looking for those who might be sympathetic to the Allied cause. As she wrote in one report, "I found a few good fields for receptions and farmers and farm hands willing and eager to help."

For reasons of security, Virginia Hall moved often, before the Gestapo or the Milice, the hated French military police, could corner her. Some agents, in fact, made it a personal rule never to stay in one house for more than two days in a row. While in France, Hall also took the precaution of always traveling with a French chaperone.

Her work took her to other small villages; she lived in the attic of a home in Cosne-Cours-sur-Loire and in the garret of a farmhouse in Sury-près-Léré. Once again her familiarity with animals played a part in her cover, as she tended a herd of goats for the farmer, giving her the opportunity to check for movement of Nazi troop carriers along country roads. In addition, delivering goat milk and cheese gave her the chance to meet farmers and workers who were willing to help her make life difficult for Hitler and his army. In one village she found a small, very trustworthy group that would

Virginia Hall sending a message on her wireless radio. The man in the background provides the power for the transmitter.

greet agents new to the country and establish three or four safe houses. Virginia Hall continued her OSS work until the end of the war, helping anti-Nazi groups with money, then with weapons and explosives to do their subversive work.

For her diligent and productive work in France, Virginia Hall was awarded the Distinguished Service Cross, the U.S. military's second most revered honor. She was the first woman to be so honored. Wild Bill Donovan thought her work deserved personal recognition from the president, so he asked Harry Truman to make the presentation himself. However, when Virginia got wind of Donovan's invitation, she asked him to reconsider involving the president. She didn't want any publicity. As she put it, she was "still operational and most anxious to get busy."

Virginia Hall continued to work in the intelligence community with the CIA, until 1966, when she retired at age sixty. She and her husband—a former OSS agent—settled on a Maryland farm, where she created much the same type of environment she had experienced as a child. She planted "thousands of bulbs" and enjoyed tending to her animals and watching birds. She also made an excellent goat cheese in the French tradition.

Spy Gadgets and Gizmos

FOR SPIES TO BE SUCCESSFUL, they need lots of support from people and equipment. False documentation and legitimate currency were two of the issues that concerned the Research and Development Section of the OSS. Agents needed authentic personal effects. To get these, the OSS created the I Cash Clothes Project. An OSS agent with a fabricated story that hid his true identity met European immigrants when their ships docked in New York Harbor. He then began his work, trading new clothes, handkerchiefs, watches, eyeglasses, key rings, and suitcases for the same items that the immigrants carried with them. (We can only imagine what the immigrants thought about America, where their old, worn possessions were replaced by new ones.) Some of the items that the OSS gathered through this project were immediately supplied to spies ready to leave for their assignments in France. Others were brought to the Research and Development Section, where they served as models for creating reproductions.

You probably wouldn't think that an agent's teeth could present a problem, but they could, if an agent had any fillings. Just as there was a difference between the quality of British clothes and French clothes, the same could be said for dental work. As a result of this disparity, the dental work of American agents needed to be altered in such a way that it looked like the work of a French dentist.

Before a new OSS agent was ready to board a plane and parachute behind enemy lines, he had to be thoroughly searched to make sure that he carried no items, no matter how innocent they seemed, that could give him away. A stick of gum, a book of matches, a picture of a sweetheart could prove to be a spy's undoing if discovered by a thorough border guard or nosy local policeman. The OSS veterans knew that the line between life and death in enemy territory was very thin indeed.

If you've watched a James Bond movie, you were probably amazed by the wild spy gadgets and gizmos that 007 has at his disposal. There was a branch of MI6 and a counterpart in the OSS that created such items for its spies. Among other things, they created a .22 caliber pistol that was silenced and emitted no muzzle flash when fired.

They also created a highly explosive powder called Aunt Jemima, because it looked like pancake mix. Blended with water or milk, the Aunt Jemima could be fashioned into bread dough that could be baked and then used to blow up a building! The R & D Section also created a highly explosive compound that looked and felt like coal. As you can imagine, these lumps of "coal" could be easily smuggled aboard an idle steam loco-motive, where they were eventually shoveled into the firebox of a locomotive as it traveled with its load of ammunition or supplies. Like the Germans in World War I who created "cigar" time bombs to sabotage Allied ships, the OSS created a barometric bomb that exploded aboard an airplane when the craft reached a specified altitude.

Since spies often need to make copies of crucial documents or take pictures of foreign agents, miniature cameras have a long history as essential pieces of spy gear. The sliding box camera is believed to be the first subminiature spy camera, from about 1865 in France.

The Super Camera was developed in the 1870s. It measures two inches wide by nearly three inches long and three inches deep.

During the latter part of the nineteenth century it was common for men to carry pocket watches. Spies and private detectives who were looking for a camera that they could easily carry and conceal were taken by the Ticka and Expo watch cameras, designed by Swedish engineer Magnus Neill. They were very popular in the early 1900s.

The Ansco Memo miniature camera was introduced in 1927. It was the only camera at the time that could take fifty pictures on one roll of film. The Memo camera, as it was called, was only about an inch and a half wide, four inches long, and two inches deep. This camera was known for taking good pictures of action and speed.

The Petal camera is another camera that was very popular with spies and undercover operatives. About the size of a quarter, it is listed in the *Guinness Book of Records* as being the smallest commercial camera ever produced.

Perhaps the most unusual spy camera was the Steineck ABC wristwatch camera, which was sold in the United States in the late 1940s and 1950s. Oddly, despite its name, this gizmo is not a functioning watch, but it did afford agents with a camera that was reasonably easy to conceal.

While all of these miniature cameras have come and gone, the Minox became the camera of choice for spies from the 1940s, when it was introduced, to the 1960s. But its popularity with spies didn't end then. In fact, John A. Walker Jr., a Soviet spy who breached United States security by photographing countless pages of secret documents and ciphers, used a newer version of the Minox. Walker's camera came with an eighteen-inch measuring chain that allowed him to easily photograph 8 x 10 inch photos and standard sheets of paper.

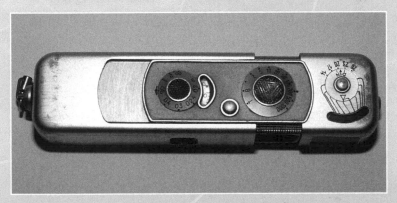

Miniature Minox camera, a favorite among spies for decades

Juan Pujol

One historian called Juan Pujol "the greatest, most remarkable double agent of World War II." He was remembered this way because he was enormously creative and successful. He was also stubbornly insistent on becoming a spy—and was very nearly passed over. Pujol was a hotel manager in his native Spain when the Nazis invaded Poland. About thirty years old at the time, Pujol was a short man, with dark receding hair that he usually wore slicked back in the style of the times. As the Nazis began their conquest of Europe, Pujol came to despise Hitler and his army of thugs. Some say that it was Hitler's treatment of the Jews that drove Pujol to make a life-changing decision to spy on the Nazis for England.

Although Pujol wanted to put his life on the line as a spy, he was too shy to offer his services at the British embassy in Madrid. Instead, he sent his wife to make the offer for him. Not surprisingly, the British rejected the offer. They were understandably leery of a walk-in—a person who volunteers his or her services as a spy—let alone one who sends his wife to offer his services.

Juan Pujol was not deterred by this rejection. If the British didn't want him as a spy, he would offer his services to Germany, hoping that if he could get the Nazis to accept

Garbo in a disguise (left) and as he normally appeared

his services, he would show himself to be a valuable asset for the British. He read whatever he could about the Nazis, all the better, as he wrote in his autobiography, to act as a "rabid Nazi supporter." Once again, however, his offer was rejected. Still, he persisted, continuing his act. "I began to use my gift of gab," he wrote, "and ranted away as befitted a staunch Nazi."

Perhaps worn down by Pujol's persistence, the Nazis agreed to send him to England as a spy. They gave him a crash course in espionage, which included superficial instructions on how to write his reports in invisible ink. He was handed a stack of British paper money, as well as an address for a mail drop where he was to send his reports. He was also given a questionnaire, a common part of a spy's travel kit, which is a list of areas of interest in England that Germany wanted Pujol to explore and report on. Finally, he was given his code name: Arabel. He left Spain in July 1941.

Then an odd thing happened. Pujol stopped in Lisbon, Portugal, once again walked into the British embassy, and once again volunteered himself as a spy. Even though he was now armed with evidence that he was working for the Germans, the British still showed no interest in his offer. So Pujol decided to stay in Lisbon and fake it. He would *pretend* to send his reports to the Abwehr, the office of German military intelligence, from England. His reports had to be mailed because he was not given a radio or even instructions on how to operate one. So, how could Arabel expect his Nazi handlers to believe that he was in England if his letters were postmarked Lisbon? Arabel concocted a story that he'd run into a pilot with Nazi loyalties who had agreed to mail his letters for him from Lisbon. For a small fee, of course.

With that part of his story in place, Arabel began gathering the props he'd need to convince the Abwehr that he was in England. First, he bought a secondhand copy of a guidebook of the U.K. and a large map of the British Isles. He also got his hands on an outdated British railway schedule. He spent many hours reading in the Lisbon library and watching current-event newsreels at a local movie theater. Beyond using such research tools, Pujol relied on his imagination.

Once he was established in his fake spy business, sending reports in invisible ink to the mail drop, Arabel found himself quite busy. So busy, in fact, that he needed other fake agents to assist him. He recruited notional—or imaginary—agents to appear to help him gather intelligence for the Fatherland. Arabel and his notional agents worked hard from late summer of 1941 into the new year. Because Germany had not been very successful establishing a spy network in the British Isles, they could not easily verify any of Arabel's reports. And even though he made some errors in his reports, the Abwehr considered him an authority on intelligence in England. On occasion, he would supply Berlin with false information that would cause them to waste valuable resources hunting for something that didn't exist. In fact, it was just such a wild goose chase that led to Arabel being "caught" by the British.

In February 1942, the British code breakers at Bletchley Park near London intercepted a message that referred to intelligence gathered by Arabel in Liverpool, England. The message mentioned a British convoy sailing from Liverpool: "fifteen ships including nine freighters, course BASTA [Gibraltar] and probably going on to Malta, possible intermediate port LISA [Lisbon]." The deciphered message caused panic in MI5. Their first thought was deeply disturbing: there was an unaccounted-for agent in the U.K. sending intelligence to Berlin. When a Bletchley agent tried to verify the convoy movement, he made a startling discovery: there was no such convoy. Yet as they tried to make sense of this intelligence, they intercepted another message from Berlin issuing an attack order to find and sink the convoy! So the Germans were spending time and fuel looking for a fifteen-ship convoy that didn't exist.

Investigators from MI5, the counter-intelligence and security agency arm of the SIS, came to believe that this rogue "spy" was none other than that slender Spaniard who had offered his services at their embassies in Spain and Portugal. But how could they find him? Luck was on their side. Arabel was tiring of his phony spy game, and, fearful that his family would get caught in the madness of war, he decided to leave Europe while he could. However, before he could put his move to Brazil into action, he made one more attempt to find a country that would welcome a new spy to its intelligence operation. This time he visited the American embassy in Lisbon, where his offer was taken more seriously. Although the Americans didn't accept his offer, they did contact the British embassy. Juan Pujol was finally on his way to being a real spy.

After a thorough investigation and a long interrogation, the British were satisfied that Pujol was Arabel. They smuggled him to England on a British steamer. Once at a safe house in the suburbs of London, Pujol was given the code name Bouril, and Tomás Harris became his case officer. The pair spent long days together for the duration of the war, continuing Bouril's work with the Nazis. Harris was pleased with Pujol's experience. "He came to us as a fully fledged double agent with all the growing pains over," the agent later wrote. "We only had to operate and develop the system that he had already set up." And develop the system they did. By the end of the war, Bouril controlled twenty-seven agents and subagents—those who work for the agents—all imaginary. In fact, Bouril did such a thorough and creative job with his agents that his code name was changed to Garbo, after one of the most popular and revered actresses of the time, Greta Garbo.

Being a top-notch double agent takes more than merely inventing characters for a play. Garbo needed to give his agents personalities, complete with character flaws. One of his notional agents, for instance, was Moonbeam, who supposedly operated in Canada and was quite the cheapskate. To make this point with the Germans, he told them that Moonbeam expected to be reimbursed for his payments to the person who shoveled snow from his front walk.

In another case, Garbo and Harris were worried that if Two, another of Garbo's agents, did not report on shipping in the Liverpool area, the Nazis might grow suspicious when their aerial reconnaissance reported shipping activity. What

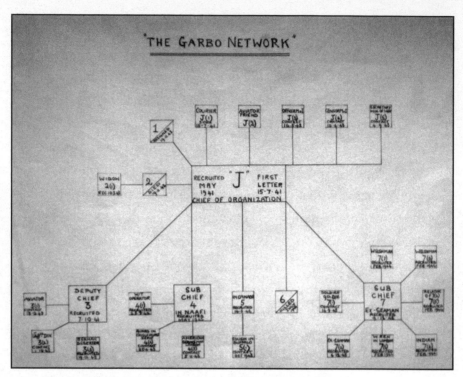

The chart Garbo used to keep track of his imaginary agents

to do? Garbo wrote to his handlers that he was worried that he hadn't heard from Two in some time. He told them that he was going to investigate. Shortly after he "arrived" in Liverpool, he learned—or so he reported—that his agent had unexpectedly died. Garbo went so far as to plant a fake obituary in the *Liverpool Daily Post:*

> GERBERS—*Nov. 19 at Bootle, after a long illness, aged 52 years, William Maximillian. Private funeral. No flowers please.*

Garbo even included this bogus announcement in one of his reports to Berlin. He asked for and received from the Germans a small compensation to the "widow Mrs. Gerbers."

If the Germans sound gullible, that's because, to a large degree, they were. So much of the intelligence from Garbo proved accurate—though not damaging to the Allies—that they believed what he reported. To avoid looking *too* perfect, Garbo would on occasion forward intelligence that proved inaccurate. One of his most successful tactics was to mail accurate intelligence at such a time that it would arrive *after* an event detailed in the report took place. One example of this technique is the information Garbo sent to divert Berlin's attention from Operation Torch, the Allied invasion of North Africa.

Late in 1942 the Allies were planning a massive landing in North Africa to take on the German troops commanded by Field Marshal Erwin Rommel, the legendary "Desert Fox." The element of surprise was crucial for the success of the landing, and Garbo played a large part in carrying out the deception. He was to send false information to the Nazis that would lead them to believe that the Allied attack would occur at a different place. Two fake operations were created to cover plans for Operation Torch. Solo 1 was a fake plan to invade Norway. Operation Overthrow featured plans for the Allies to invade the north coast of France, the same area, as it turned out, of Operation Overlord, the D-day invasion two years later.

Garbo reported fabricated information that "proved" that the Allies were ready to invade Norway. For example, he wrote that Allied command had ordered 20,000 shoulder patches with *Norge* embroidered on them. They were to be delivered to resistance fighters in Norway. He reported other "facts" that pointed to action in a cold country: that the Allies had ordered large amounts of anti-freeze and snow chains for their invasion vehicles, that they were investigating the availability of Norwegian currency at large banks, and that they were requiring junior officers to take a class in mountain warfare.

With intelligence like this provided by one of their best agents, the Germans had no reason for doubt. As a result of such information, the Germans shifted troops and equipment from Africa to Norway and northern France, exactly what the Allies had hoped for. The diverted troops could not return to North Africa in time to help their comrades.

To make sure that Germany continued to think highly of Garbo's intelligence, he mailed a report that included the details of Operation Torch. However, he timed the letter to arrive *after* the northern Africa invasion had begun. Garbo and his handlers knew that his letter would arrive too late to help the Germans or compromise the invasion yet would still show Berlin that Garbo had in the end been able to obtain accurate information. The Germans seemed satisfied, even though the final, correct information had arrived too late to be actionable.

The Germans finally allowed Garbo to transmit his information on a radio, which cut out much of the tedium of writing a report in invisible ink. Nonetheless, Garbo and Harris continued to spend many hours making sure that their messages said just what they wanted them to say. In the three years of his work with MI5, Garbo worked like a man possessed. In his book *The Deceivers,* Thaddeus Holt describes a typical day for Garbo this way: "Harris and GARBO would meet each day, devising false information, composing messages, inventing new imaginary subagents, breaking occasionally for lunch or dinner . . . and beyond question having the times of their lives."

OSS Training

BECAUSE THE U.S. HAD NO TRAINING FACILITIES for spies at the start of World War II, it took some months before training camps were ready in this country. Training, however, could not wait, so early OSS agents were trained at Camp X, not too far from Toronto, Canada. This camp, the first secret-agent training camp in North America, was established by the British to assist their American allies. Eventually eight training bases were established in the United States, all near Baltimore, Maryland, and Washington, D.C. One facility, in fact, at an abandoned boys camp, later became Camp David, a retreat for U.S. presidents.

OSS agents-in-training worked in the various camps, which specialized in aspects of espionage, before going to something of a finishing school for spies at "The Farm," a sprawling one-hundred-acre estate in Maryland, about twenty miles south of Washington. On the Farm they learned the skills they would need to stay alive behind enemy lines. Agents learned how to use weapons and were trained in close-up and hand-to-hand combat—a combination of jujitsu and what the instructor called "Gutter Fighting." One agent recalled that he learned how to dislocate someone's arm while holding a knife under his ribs. He told his students: "You're interested only in disabling or killing your enemy. . . . There's no fair play; no rules except one: kill or be killed." The instructor's favorite weapon was a razor-sharp stiletto, "a silent, deadly weapon. . . . Never mind the blood. Just take care of it quickly."

To help them transmit their messages, they received instructions about codes and ciphers, as well as how to operate a radio transmitter. All spies were given a well-conceived legend, or cover story. They learned how to use their cover story and fake identity cards. The students at the Farm learned other practical skills, like how to pick a lock, how to parachute safely, and how to inflate a rubber boat, often their means of entering a country or leaving it.

Since the agents would be working behind enemy lines, they were schooled in sabotage. They learned how to use explosives to destroy locomotives, power-plant turbines, communication centers, and telephone systems. They learned to disable railroad cars by removing the grease in the gearboxes and by putting sugar in gasoline tanks to destroy engines.

Of course, no schooling is complete without a final exam, and the Farm was no exception. Each of the aspiring spies had to prove to their instructors that they could survive and gather meaningful intelligence. Each was given an assignment that involved working for one week as an undercover agent in a U.S. area that was similar to one controlled by the Allies, such as England, and conduct a brief mission gathering intelligence or creating an opportunity for sabotage. One assignment—or scheme, as it was known—called for a team of three agents to work in one of the East-Coast industrial cities that was not too far from the Farm: Baltimore, Richmond, or Philadelphia. The team was to find a defense plant that was guarded by the FBI and "blow it up." Actually, they had to breach plant security and place a note on the plant's main boiler that said, "This is a bomb." Once they were safely away from the factory, they called the FBI and reported their "bomb." Some of the teams that were unsuccessful in their sabotage were punched and beaten before the FBI agents called OSS to see if the "saboteurs" were really working for the OSS.

Another scheme was more complicated. Using false identity cards produced at the Farm, agents were expected to get inside secure defense plants or similar sensitive operations. Once inside, they were to get their hands on some sensitive information, sneak it out of the plant, and transmit the secret material to colleagues in code.

One agent acquired letterhead stationery from a famous Hollywood studio and wrote a letter to the manager of a steel mill, explaining that the agent was interested in making a short film about the contribution that the plant was making to the war effort. When the agent showed up at the steel mill, he invited the manager and his wife to dinner. As the agent said years later, "He wined and dined me, I wined and dined him." No one bothered to check his credentials to make sure that he was, in fact, representing the movie studio.

A group of agents-in-training was sent to Baltimore. As trainee Ed Weismiller put it, "We were simply to come back with as much information as we could about what was going on that had to do with the war effort. If we got in trouble, they didn't know us." Weismiller decided to visit the Baltimore and Ohio Railroad yard, figuring there would be plenty of war-related activities there.

He arrived at the yard, confident of his legend. He played the part of a writer. "With any lie," he said, "you learned to make it as close to the truth as possible." The B&O officials were pleased that he'd chosen to write about their railroad. They asked for his ID, which was normally prepared by a railroad security officer. Acting embarrassed, he told them that he had spilled coffee on it (and on his shirt). He had changed his shirt, but he'd neglected to pick up his ID. But he promised to bring it with him the next day. The ID was never mentioned again.

After deftly handling the problem with his ID card, Weismiller had the run of the facilities. In fact, he was given a car and a driver, as well as a photographer to work with him. According to Weismiller, when the trio arrived at a secure area, he was told that, although he wasn't supposed to be in such an area, "surely there's no harm" if he looked around. Weismiller recalls collecting "notebooks full of information" that he should not have had access to. One lesson he learned: "Just being a nice guy could get you into the most sensitive areas." He returned to the Farm and shocked everyone with his stack of intelligence. Weismiller had passed his final exam.

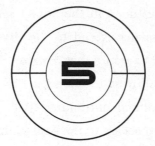

Cold War Spies

When World War II ended in Europe in 1945, the victorious Allies, as part of the peace treaty, divided Germany into four parts — one each for the United States, England, France, and Russia. The Soviet Union gained control of the eastern part of the country, while the other three Allied nations controlled the western part. (Eventually these sections became East Germany and West Germany, respectively.) This division of the country was also duplicated in the capital city of Berlin, with the Allied section in the western part of the city and the Soviet section in the east.

But Berlin was deep in the Soviet section of Germany. Although the Russians agreed to the division of Berlin in 1944, they refused to assure that the Americans, French, and British would be allowed to enter the city. Tension between the two sides escalated until June 1948, when the Soviets blocked all western access to the capital. In this first real crisis of the Cold War, the West was not going to be denied by the Soviets. Since such tension was typical in the divided city, it should come as no surprise that Berlin in the early 1950s was a city of intrigue, espionage, and danger.

An uneasy peace prevailed between the Russians and the other Allies, but each side was suspicious of the other. The United States wanted desperately to know what the Soviets were thinking. The big fear for the U.S. was that the Soviets would attack West Germany without warning, or in diplomatic language, with "a cold start." The U.S. knew that the Soviets possessed nuclear weapons. Would they use them on the West? This question and others would need to be answered by U.S. intelligence agents.

The Berlin Tunnel

The U.S. recognized that the best intelligence was firsthand intelligence, like that gathered through decrypted messages.

Intercepted messages provided information that was not colored by the spy who gathered it. Having no success planting a spy in East Berlin, U.S. intelligence was at a loss about how to penetrate the Soviet sector of the city. So, in February 1954, members of the CIA met with members of MI6, Britain's intelligence agency, at a posh London townhouse. Among those present at the meeting were Peter Lunn, head of MI6's Berlin station; George Blake, a member of MI6's Y Section, which concentrated on the Soviet threat; and William King Harvey, the CIA's head of station in Berlin.

After much discussion, the conversation turned to the idea of digging a tunnel to reach and tap the Soviet phone lines in Berlin. Some historians credit Harvey with the brainstorm, but the British must have had a hand in it as well. In 1949 the British had executed Operation Silver in Vienna when Peter Lunn was the British head of station. They had dug three tunnels to tap the Soviet lines. The longest tunnel in Operation Silver was only seventy feet long. The one in Berlin would need to be twenty times longer.

Never short on self-assurance, the rotund Harvey would direct the digging of a similar tunnel in Berlin, a project in which the British SIS would assist. The U.S. would be responsible for digging the tunnel itself, and the British would dig the vertical shaft to reach the cables that were the target of the operation. They would also provide an expert to connect the actual tap. The CIA called its part of the operation Gold. The British called their part Stopwatch.

The CIA planning was extraordinary. Questions were asked. Problems were anticipated, solutions suggested. With information provided by an informant in the Soviet state-run telephone operation, the U.S. knew that the spot they needed to reach with the tunnel was under Schönefelder Chaussee, a major highway that ran along the southern edge of Berlin. Running along the highway was a fence that separated the Soviet sector from the American sector. On the other side of the fence lay a large vacant lot that would be the starting point of the Berlin tunnel. The U.S. Corps of Engineers would build three large warehouses on this property, and from inside one of the warehouses they would begin digging the tunnel. To reach the target beneath Schönefelder Chaussee, the tunnel needed to be about 1,500 feet long, roughly as long as five football fields. Engineers figured that a six-foot-high tunnel of that length would displace about three thousand tons of sandy soil.

The planning reached this point before someone asked how they would dispose of so much soil. Trucking it out would arouse the curiosity of the suspicious Soviet guards patrolling along the fence. Then someone at the meeting said, half in jest, that they should dig a hole and bury it. But how can you bury a mountain of soil? Before long, the army engineers came up with a plan that would allow them to do just that. And it would involve one of the other of the three warehouses.

Construction work on the warehouses began in December 1953. The U.S. made no attempts to disguise their building project. In fact, they even hired German contractors to do some of the work. There was nothing unusual about two of the buildings, but on the roof of the warehouse closest to the road, the U.S. installed a set of parabolic antennas to create the impression that it was a listening post, thus offering an explanation for the barbed-wire-topped fence that enclosed the property. This building also had a full cellar hole dug. The engineers explained to the German workers that the deep cellar would give them extra storage space. In reality, what the engineers planned to store in the cellar was three thousand tons of soil!

To make sure that the design of the tunnel was sound, the Army Corps of Engineers built a 450-foot tunnel with the same design at the White Sands Proving Ground in New Mexico. The digging went well, but to ensure that the longer tunnel in Berlin would hold up, the army decided to line it with six-foot curved steel plates that engineers used in building huge dams in the western United States.

By September 1954, the warehouse construction was complete. The digging equipment was ready. So were the men who were going to work on the tunnel for the next four months. The first step in the operation was to dig a vertical shaft eighteen feet across and twenty feet deep. From the end of the shaft, the engineers turned east and dug a six-and-a-half-foot-high horizontal tunnel. They dug with hand tools, advancing slowly, erecting slats along the way to prevent a cave-in. When one section of the tunnel was dug, the slats were removed and the tunnel was reinforced with 125 tons of three-inch-thick curved steel plates, jammed into place, then bolted together. To strengthen the tunnel, a thousand cubic yards of concrete had been pumped into the space between the steel plates and the dirt walls.

The Americans knew that the Soviets were watching them as the warehouses were being built, so they needed to be careful not to do anything that would tip off the Soviets to the true purpose of the construction. Before the digging had progressed very far, someone raised a security issue: what would happen if the Soviets noticed that the "engineers" who were working on the project, emerged from the buildings covered in dirt? Would that be a red flag for the Soviets? The U.S. wasn't taking any chances. They had a washer and a dryer installed in the warehouse so the diggers could wash their uniforms before leaving the warehouse.

The next problem that the diggers faced involved the water table, the point where the ground becomes saturated with water. Engineers calculated where the tunnel could extend without the danger of hitting the water table. But when water started seeping into the tunnel, they knew that they had miscalculated. The tunnel needed to be elevated enough to avoid the possibility of flooding. But such a maneuver would bring the tunnel uncomfortably close to the road. The decision was made to continue. The project had gone too far to stop.

Finally, on February 28, 1954, the tunnel was complete. When the diggers reached the spot directly below their target cables, they had removed 3,100 tons of dirt and completed a 1,476-foot tunnel. But completion brought a new worry: what if noise from the activity in the tunnel reached the street? After all, the tunnel was only eighteen inches below the surface of Schönefelder Chaussee. Solution: the tunnel was lined with sandbags to muffle any sounds. The sandbags also offered a convenient shelf to hold power and signal cables.

Then it was time for SIS to do their part. It took the British eighteen days to complete their work digging the "tap chamber," a small room where the cables would actually be tapped. A reinforced concrete roof was added to the room to prevent the roadway from breaking through under the weight of passing traffic. When the chamber was sound, SIS agent John Wyke took over. Those who worked with Wyke remembered him as a smooth ballroom dancer and quite the ladies' man. But MI6 also knew him to be a veteran of many missions for the SOE, having worked in the Middle East for most of the war. Most

Sandbags line the walls of the Berlin spy tunnel.

important for this operation, John Wyke was the SIS's phone tapping expert.

Wyke's work was always delicate and demanding, more so in the damp and confined space. Gently and carefully, Wyke scraped the dirt until he found the three cables encased in black rubber and, he believed, pressurized by nitrogen, a common practice in the 1950s to keep moisture out of cables. He knew that once he cut through the rubber sheathing on the cables, the nitrogen would escape. The resulting drop in pressure would be detected by the Soviets. The engineers solved this potential problem by building a concrete barrier with a steel door to pressurize the tap chamber and separate it from the pre-amp room. (It turned out that the cables were not pressurized.)

Wkye next attached wires to the exposed cable—probably with alligator clips—and began to draw power from the cables. Once again, the work called for a deft hand. If he drew off too much power, the Soviets would be sure to notice it. As expected, Wkye did a masterful job, and the tapping began on May 11, 1955.

Because the signals coming from the taps were weak, they needed to be amplified. So from the tap chamber they were fed into the next section of the tunnel, which was filled with delicate electronic equipment. (This heavy equipment was moved slowly down the tunnel by a forklift with a converted electric motor over wooden tracks.) The near end of the pre-amp chamber was fitted with a torch-proof steel door set in a thick concrete wall. The door was alarmed and fortified with a lock and a slide bar. Near the door hung a sign that read ENTRY IS FORBIDDEN BY ORDER OF THE COMMANDING GENERAL. Bill Harvey made it policy that the door was to be locked at all times except when people were in the chamber. A telephone connected the chamber to the operation center in the warehouse.

The scope of the operation is staggering. The three cables, carrying 1,200 communication channels, yielded over 50,000 reels of recording tape, or, put another way, twenty-five tons of tape. These tapes were flown to London for analysis. At its peak, the SIS Main Processing Office in London employed three hundred workers who recorded 75,000 conversations and fully transcribed 17,000 of them. The daily output of printed transcript pages, if bound into books, would make a stack 10 feet wide, 15 feet deep, and 8 feet high! The Washington, D.C., team recorded 18,000 six-hour tape reels

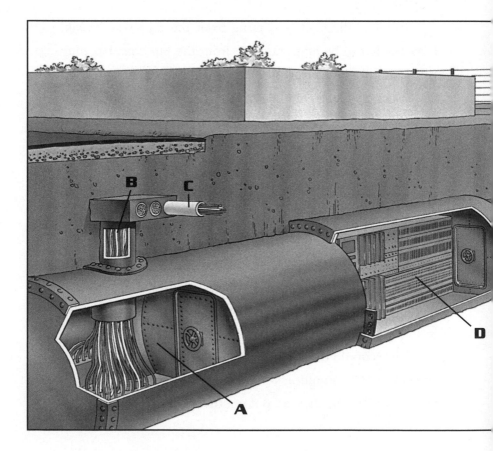

of German Teletype messages. Each tape could hold more than two hundred hours of messages.

But as Allen Dulles, director of the CIA at the time of the tunnel construction, wrote in *The Craft of Intelligence,* "Most intelligence operations have a limited span of usefulness. . . . This is assumed when the project starts." He and the operatives had no idea, of course, how long the tunnel's usefulness

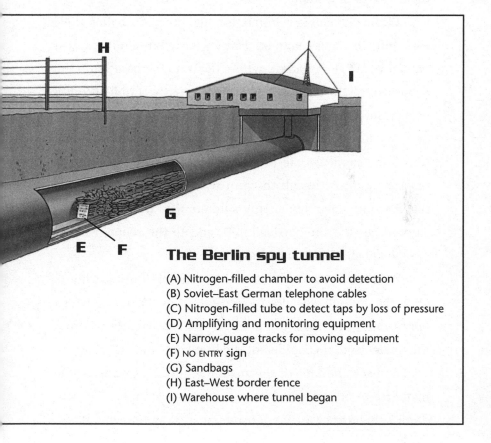

The Berlin spy tunnel

(A) Nitrogen-filled chamber to avoid detection
(B) Soviet–East German telephone cables
(C) Nitrogen-filled tube to detect taps by loss of pressure
(D) Amplifying and monitoring equipment
(E) Narrow-guage tracks for moving equipment
(F) NO ENTRY sign
(G) Sandbags
(H) East–West border fence
(I) Warehouse where tunnel began

would last. Its lifespan turned out to be eleven months and eleven days.

On April 22, 1958, Bill Harvey woke to the sound of his telephone ringing. As soon as he heard the words, "We've got a problem," he bolted from bed and raced to the warehouse and into the tunnel. The Soviets had discovered the tunnel. All the technicians had been evacuated from their posts at the first sign of trouble.

While the Soviets toiled for ten hours to batter their way into the tap chamber, Harvey ordered sandbags and barbed wire to be piled up where the tunnel crossed into the American sector of Berlin. Harvey hurriedly scribbled out a sign in German on a scrap of cardboard that read, *You are now entering the American sector*. When the sign was propped up on the sandbags, he ordered his men to set up a heavy machine gun. Although the gun was not loaded, he hoped that it would deter any enemy soldiers who were tempted to explore beyond the barricade. To add to the scene, Harvey crouched behind the machine gun.

At three o'clock that afternoon—nearly fourteen hours after the tunnel was discovered—Harvey heard footsteps approaching from the direction of the tap chamber. Before the Soviet soldiers could spot the barricade and sign, Harvey yanked back the bolt of the machine gun. Its unmistakable metallic sound echoed down the tunnel, stopping the soldiers in their tracks. After a brief pause, they retreated down the tunnel. Within thirty minutes the Soviets had cut the tap cables. One of the linguists muttered, "It's gone." Indeed, it was. After running for eleven months and eleven days, Operation Gold/Stopwatch was finished.

What the CIA and SIS did not know is that George Blake, the SIS agent who had arrived to work at the Berlin station, was a Soviet mole. Blake was the Y Section agent who attended the February 1954 MI6–CIA meeting in London. Two days after the meeting, Blake met with his Soviet handler. As Blake later wrote, "I handed to him film of the minutes taken at the meetings together with the accompanying sketches and plans which I had been able to photograph in my office during lunchtime the previous day." Blake also reported that his handler was impressed by the scope and boldness of the plan. In fact, the handler "asked me to meet him again soon so that we could discuss it in more detail and I could keep him informed of any fresh developments."

Not only did Blake keep the Soviets current on the tunnel, but he also continued to work for them until he was arrested by British intelligence agents in 1961. After serving almost six years of his forty-two-year sentence, he escaped. The Soviets smuggled him out of England, and he eventually wound up living in Moscow.

The question remains: since the Soviets knew about the tunnel, why did they let it go on for nearly a year before making a big show of "discovering" it? And if they knew the

Americans were tapping their communications, were they simply feeding the CIA disinformation? And if they were, how could the project have been worth its $25 million to $30 million price tag?

As you might expect, there are many divergent assessments of the success of the operation. One Western intelligence officer called it a "bonanza to Western counterintelligence specialists." But a CIA operative of the era offered his opinion of the intelligence gathered via the tunnel: "Whether it was sexy, hold-your-breath data, I tend to doubt it."

There are theories as to why the Soviets did not "discover" the tunnel sooner. One likely answer is that they waited until Blake was reassigned by MI6 to London in order to protect him from being found out. Since Blake knew about the tunnel from the first day of its planning and was in Berlin while the tunnel was being dug, fingers would soon point to him as a Soviet mole. The KGB did not want to lose Blake. Some historians feel that the KGB waited because they actually wanted the Americans to hear their transmissions, as a way to let it be known that Russia had no intention of invading Germany and going to war with the U.S.

On balance, however, some valuable information was gathered from the tapped conversations. The U.S. learned, for example, a great deal about the Soviet and Eastern European order of battle, or its military organization. Others feel that the intelligence was valuable to check against similar information obtained from other sources. Tim Weiner in his recent history of the CIA, *Legacy of Ashes,* writes that "The evidence suggests that the CIA gained two invaluable and untainted kinds of knowledge from the taps. The agency learned a basic blueprint of the Soviet and East German security systems, and it never picked up a glimmer of warning that Moscow intended to go to war."

The Berlin tunnel did not alter the course of the Cold War, despite the efforts of the Soviet propaganda frenzy. In 1961, the Soviets built the Berlin Wall, separating East Berlin from West Berlin. The wall, and the Cold War, lasted nearly thirty more years, until 1989. On November 9, after a peaceful demonstration against the totalitarian government, East Germans began tearing down the wall. Unlike in the past, however, the Soviets did not intervene with force. Mikhail Gorbachev, the reform-minded head of the USSR, decided that the problem of reuniting Germany was best left to the German people.

One-Time Pad

DURING THE COLD WAR, U.S. code breakers worked diligently at Arlington Hall, Virginia—a former girls school across the Potomac River from Washington, D.C.—on intercepted Soviet messages, knowing that breaking a code is usually the product of hard work, playing hunches, and a little luck. Such was the case when Cecil Phillips, a code breaker at Arlington Hall, realized that the messages were double-enciphered. In other words, the message was enciphered, and then *that* enciphered message was again enciphered by another method, called a one-time pad. Each sheet in the pad was filled with columns of random five-digit numbers that the sender and receiver of a secret message would use to add another layer of difficulty to their messages.

To use a one-time pad, a sender enciphers a message by "translating" each word of the message, called the plaintext, into a group of five-digit "words" that are found in his codebook. Let's say that the first word in the plaintext is EXTREME, and the codebook's equivalent is 37857. If the sender stopped there, that in itself would present a tough but breakable system for the code breakers. But here's where the one-time pad is used. The "word" 37857 is added to the first group of random digits on the one-time pad, say

11961. The addition of those two numbers was made using what is called Fibonacci arithmetic, in which numbers greater that 9 are not carried over. So, 37857 + 11961 = 48718, and *that* is what the sender transmits as the first word of the message. If the next "word" of the plaintext message is 65237 (for DANGER), that number is added to the *second* group of random numbers on the one-time pad, and so on through the entire message. When the sender and receiver of a secret message were finished with their work, the sheet they used for it was destroyed, thus creating an unbreakable code. The next sheet was used for the next message, and so on.

In *Spycatcher*, Peter Wright, former assistant director of MI5, offers a "very close approximation of the kind of challenge we were faced with" at Arlington Hall:

TEXT OF MESSAGE
YOUR COMMUNICATION OF 74689 AND 02985
47199 67789 88005 62971 CONCERNING SPELL
H I C K S ENDSPELL 55557 81045 10835 68971
71129 EXTREME CAUTION AT PRESENT TIME 56690
12748 92640 00471 SPELL S T A N L E Y ENDSPELL
37106 72885 MONTHLY UNTIL FURTHER NOTICE.
SIGNATURE OF MESSAGE

Each page of a one-time pad was used for a different message.

After deciphering many intercepts, Arlington Hall created a long list of code names and tradecraft words, such as:

ARSENAL: U.S. War Department

BABYLON: San Francisco

THE BANK: Department of State

BOAR: Winston Churchill

CARTHAGE: Washington, D.C.

COUNTRY: United States

ISLAND: Great Britain

KAPITAN: President Roosevelt

PUT ON ICE or IN COLD STORAGE: deactivate an agent

The U-2 Spy Plane

As the drama of the Berlin tunnel played out, there were people in the U.S. government who continued to see the Soviet Union as a threat to the United States. Influenced by Soviet propaganda and scant factual evidence, parts of the U.S. government were convinced that there was a "bomber gap" between Russia and America. They believed that the Soviets possessed a large fleet of long-range bombers that could reach America's shores and wipe out U.S. cities and military installations. Those who believed in this wide imbalance in offensive weapons were pressing President Dwight Eisenhower to do something about it. Eisenhower, never convinced that such a bomber gap existed, nevertheless agreed that the military did need credible evidence about the military capabilities of the Soviet Union. At the same time, he believed in working for better relations with the Soviets.

In April 1953, the RAND Corporation, a Washington, D.C., think tank, issued an impact report that stated "the enemy will have the capability that many in the U.S. military and intelligence communities already believe, that the U.S. has not kept pace with advances in military technologies." Further, the study reported that the United States suffered from gaps in intelligence gathering. "Our intelligence tells us essentially nothing" about Soviet plans and capabilities, the report declared. To avoid "another Pearl Harbor," the United States needed to begin to close the intelligence gap as quickly as possible. Richard Helms, former CIA director, recalled that there was "an extraordinary absence of knowledge" in the intelligence committee about the Soviet military. Lawrence Houston, the CIA's general counsel at the time, recalled later that the lack of intelligence "was just appalling." To make matters worse, the world learned that the Soviets had tested its first thermonuclear bomb on August 12, 1953.

It was in this atmosphere of fear and uncertainty that Eisenhower gave permission in 1954 for the CIA to design and build a spy plane. He gave this order with reluctance, fearing that such a spy plane could actually precipitate a Soviet attack. The group that would execute the project consisted of many of the country's brightest engineers, scientists, businessmen, and government officials. They set up shop in Burbank, California, at Lockheed Aircraft Company. Before long, the group referred to its offices and labs in an aircraft hangar as Skunk Works because they had to keep everybody away from their work.

The men of Skunk Works decided that if the spy plane had any chance of avoiding detection as it flew its secret missions, it needed to fly high enough and fast enough to avoid Soviet surface-to-air missiles and any fighter planes sent to intercept

A U-2 spy plane

it and shoot it down. Of course, it needed a sophisticated camera system that would take the pictures that would provide reliable intelligence. Last, the plane needed to be designed, built, and tested as quickly as possible and in utmost secrecy.

In short, the design group set out to build the most advanced espionage device ever created. If they could do it, the plane could very well prevent war between the United States and the Soviet Union.

The task before Clarence L. "Kelly" Johnson, a brilliant airplane designer for Lockheed, and his staff was staggering. The plane had to be able to reach a maximum speed of about 500 miles per hour, have a range of 2,200 miles,and a ceiling of about 13 miles (70,000 feet). But that mandate created mechanical as well as design challenges. Edwin Land, brilliant inventor (of among other things, the Polaroid camera) was responsible for the design. One historian wrote that Land envisioned a subsonic jet adapted from sailplane designs.

If the mechanics of the U-2 were groundbreaking, the design was even more controversial. The body of the aircraft was about 50 feet long, but the wingspan was almost 80 feet. The original U-2 had a landing gear like a bicycle wheel, a tail wheel and a single main wheel beneath the body of the plane, located just ahead of the wing. In addition to the landing gear, the U-2 had a wheel at the end of each long, flexible wing. However, because designers wanted the craft to be as light as possible, these wheels were released after the plane was airborne! Without these wing wheels, landing the U-2 was challenging and dangerous, requiring the pilot to touch down on the landing gears, then carefully and gently tip the plane to one side until the wing tip dragged on the ground and slowed down the plane.

While a team of Skunk Works engineers worked on creating a spy plane, another team worked on the cameras. After all, the whole point of the project was to obtain clear pictures. The cameras needed to do two things: take panoramic pictures as well as high-resolution shots of specific targets. In an early model, two cameras were used. One was mounted in a way that looked directly below the aircraft, while the other swiveled left and right to take panoramic shots. In an attempt to reduce the weight of the plane, a second design used just one camera, which took pictures from several overlapping positions, moving from horizon to horizon for panoramic pictures. At the same time, when the camera focused on scenes directly below the aircraft, it produced remarkably clear pictures. From an altitude of nearly eleven miles, the camera could capture objects as small as thirty inches wide, roughly the size of the top of your refrigerator. The camera could record a 125-mile swath of land on a single strip of film.

To convince Eisenhower that the camera could do exactly what the CIA and the designers said it could do, they sent a test flight directly over the president's farm in Gettysburg, Pennsylvania, and photographed his cows from more than ten miles high. When the initial flights over the

Soviet Union began, the early pictures were of the Kremlin and Soviet premier Nikita Khrushchev's summer home, driving home the point to Eisenhower that the spy plane could go, in a sense, right where the Russians lived.

As design of the U-2 continued a bit ahead of schedule, the CIA worked on recruiting pilots for the dangerous spy missions. The best pilots were in the air force, but because of the sensitive and politically explosive nature of spy flights over the Soviet Union, the president refused to allow active military pilots to fly the U-2s. If something should go amiss, he did not want the project to look like a military operation. So the CIA identified the best air force pilots, who were then allowed to resign from military service. As civilians, they were free to be hired by the CIA. This process of hiring former air force pilots was called "sheep dipping," a reference to a process in which sheep were dipped in disinfectants to kill parasites.

A third group of engineers set to work on a flight suit that would protect U-2 pilots. The engineers well knew the damage that could be done to the human body at such high altitudes. At 65,000 feet, bodily fluids, blood included, vaporize. In addition, the cardiovascular system is placed under tremendous stress. Although the cabin of the U-2 was pressurized—just like the cabin of a commercial jet airliner—engineers were concerned that they needed to do more to protect the pilot. They needed to build a flight suit that would save the pilot if he needed to bail out at such high altitudes.

Since a person's body can actually expand at high pressure, the main function of the suit was to keep the body from stretching to a deadly level. The cotton-and-nylon suits were custom built to fit individual pilots. The suit was lined with inflatable tubes that would expand at a drop in air pressure. These air-filled tubes kept the body from expanding. The suits were modified as new information was gained from test flights. For example, an expandable chest bladder was added to help the pilots breathe more naturally if the pressure dropped. This bladder was later expanded to cover the upper part of the body.

Working around the clock with a spirit of cooperation frequently absent in government projects, the U-2 project was completed in eighteen months from concept to delivered product. More remarkable, perhaps, than completing the project well before the deadline was that it was completed under budget.

The first U-2 flight occurred in July 1956; the plane returned with remarkable pictures that began to show that the fears of some in government were unfounded. There was no "bomber gap." Nor were the Soviets leading in the arms race. The flights continued, always with the direct approval of the president for each one. Over the next four years, the CIA flew twenty-four U-2 missions over the Soviet Union, some from bases in England and Germany, others from bases closer to the Soviet Union, such as in Pakistan. The CIA estimates that by the time the U-2 program ended in 1960, the planes had produced 1,285,000 feet of film that covered nearly 1.3 million square miles of the Soviet Union, about 15 percent of the nation's landmass.

With the deluge of photos taken from ten to twelve miles in the sky—higher still when spy satellite surveillance began in the 1960s—the CIA established the Photographic Intelligence Division (PID), whose job was to make measurements using photography. In addition, the analysts of PID compared pictures of the same area taken weeks apart, looking for any changes such as ongoing construction of landing fields, hangars, or rocket launch towers. Their keen eyes searched for the smallest clue that the Russians were preparing to use long-range bombers or missiles.

Despite the success of the intelligence gathered from the flights, President Eisenhower was never at ease with the missions even though he was led to believe by the CIA that the U-2s were virtually invisible. But the agency knew differently. In fact, it had received information two days after the first flight that Russian radar had, in fact, detected the spy plane and had made several unsuccessful attempts to shoot it down. Nonetheless, the flights continued and thousands of intelligence photos were processed and analyzed.

The CIA assured the president that even if the U-2 was intercepted, the chances of the plane and its pilot surviving a ten-mile fall to earth were practically zero. In fact, safeguards were in place to make sure that neither man nor machine survived a missile strike so that no information about the design and function of the U-2 could be gathered by Russia. Every pilot carried poison pins coated with shellfish toxin. A jab of the pin would kill the pilot. In addition, each U-2 included an explosive charge under the pilot's seat. Should the pilot need to eject from the aircraft, he would set the charge, which would destroy the plane, its instruments, and the camera in seventy seconds after the pilot ejected. Richard Bissell, the director of the project, told Eisenhower that it "would be *impossible,* if things should go wrong, for the Soviets to come in possession of the equipment intact."

After four years of successful flights of the U-2, the CIA's luck ran out in the spring of 1960. In April, a U-2 flight over Tyuratam, in what is now Kazakhstan, took pictures of a site that analysts found suspicious. Although the site was under construction, it looked like a launch area for large missiles that could reach the United States. The CIA desperately requested a U-2 mission to get a better look at the site. Bissell pressed the president, who finally and reluctantly agreed to one more flight.

On May 1, 1960, Francis Gary Powers, a sheep-dipped air force pilot, powered his U-2 into the sky from a runway in Peshawar, in northern Pakistan. His flight plan called for him to fly across a western part of the Soviet Union before he landed in Norway. About four hundred miles into Soviet airspace, his U-2 was shot down. Despite all the precautions installed to destroy the plane and the pilot, Powers and the remains of the plane fell to earth near Sverdlovsk. He was quickly surrounded by villagers and turned over to the KGB.

Although the CIA knew that Soviet radar had detected the high-flying spy plane, the agency felt that neither the Soviet jet fighters nor its missile could catch up with the U-2. Powers himself testified that he had "no idea what happened." He further testified, "I heard and felt a hollow-sounding explosion. It seemed to be behind me and I could see orange-colored light." Historians seem to agree that the U-2 "flamed out," meaning that its engine cut out in the thin atmosphere of 70,000 feet. Such a flameout is often accompanied by an explosion of gases at the plane's tail.

As the plane started to tumble out of control, Powers was afraid that he would lose his legs if he fired the ejection seat. Fighting centrifugal force, he pushed back the canopy. However, the resulting loss of pressure triggered his flight suit to inflate, just as it had been designed to do. But, with the suit inflated, he could no longer reach the switch to activate the charge that would destroy the plane. When the tube to his oxygen mask pulled loose, Powers was free of the plane. His parachute opened at the prescribed altitude, and he floated to earth.

As soon as news of the missing plane reached the White House, where it was assumed that both plane and pilot were lost, the administration began preemptive damage control. The story they spun was that a U.S. weather plane was missing over the Soviet Union. The administration suggested that the pilot had become disoriented after a malfunction of the oxygen system. Even as the spin was fed to the world's media, the Soviets were preparing a surprise for our government.

Unbeknownst to the Eisenhower administration, the Russians had not only captured Powers but they had also recovered a large section of the plane, as well as cameras and other equipment, including the pilot's survival kit, which included Russian money, as well as women's jewelry and men's watches to win favor with his captors. Because Powers was immediately taken captive, he had no opportunity to use the survival kit as part of his escape. Nor did he have time to take his life with the poison pin that was part of his kit.

Nikita Khrushchev, premier of the Soviet Union, waited to see how the United States would respond to the loss of their aircraft over Soviet soil. When the U.S. issued its fabricated tale of the purpose of the flight, Khrushchev sprang his trap. On May 7, 1960, he revealed to the Supreme Soviet what he knew about the flight. "I must tell you a secret," he

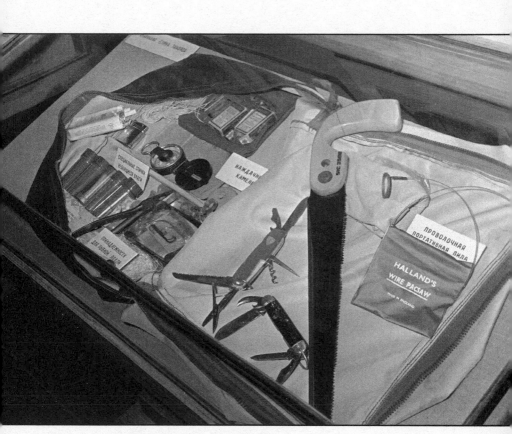

The pilot's emergency pack from Powers's U-2

said. "When I was making my report, I deliberately did not say that the pilot was alive and in good health . . . And now, just look how many silly things [the Americans] have said." His statement shone the light of truth on the American pronouncement that "there was no authorization for any such flight" from Washington.

The political fallout from the U-2 incident came the following week, when Eisenhower and Khrushchev were to meet in Paris for a long-awaited summit meeting. When the president refused to apologize for the violation of international law with U.S. spy planes, Khrushchev walked out of the talks and the summit abruptly ended.

Francis Gary Powers pleaded guilty in a Soviet court on August 17, 1960, and was convicted of espionage. His life was spared, but he was sentenced to three years imprisonment and seven years of hard labor. After serving a year and a half of his sentence, he was freed from a Soviet jail in a prisoner swap. In return for Powers's release, the U.S. turned over Rudolf Abel, a Russian spy serving time in an American prison.

The end of the age of the U-2 did not, however, mean the end of American surveillance of Soviet military facilities. Work on a spy satellite, code-named Corona, was increased. In the meantime, the U.S. deployed a supersonic spy plane, Oxcart, to continue surveillance. Corona was an operational space surveillance system for thirteen years, until 1972, taking pictures with a 70-degree panoramic camera that filmed by scanning at a right angle to the path of the aircraft. The list of surveillance accomplishments of the Corona is long, including imaging all Soviet medium-range, intermediate-range, and intercontinental missile facilities and determining the exact locations of Soviet air defense missile batteries.

There is an ironic final chapter to the U-2 story. Fifteen years after the spy swap brought Francis Gary Powers back to the United States, he began work as a traffic helicopter pilot for a television station in Los Angeles. On August 1, 1977, he was killed when his helicopter crashed.

Eavesdropping in Moscow

IN 1945, IN A TOUCHING ACT OF FRIENDSHIP, a group of Soviet schoolchildren presented a two-foot, hand-carved wooden replica of the Great Seal of the United States to the American ambassador W. Averell Harriman. As a sign of his gratitude for the gift, Harriman hung the Great Seal in his office in Spaso House, the ambassador's residence in Moscow.

The Great Seal hung on the wall for seven years until ambassador George Kennan took up residence at Spaso House. It was only then that a routine security check revealed a shocking secret buried in the wooden seal. A hidden microphone had broadcast all conversations that had taken place in the ambassador's office.

Kennan explained in his memoirs how the tiny microphone was found in the carved eagle. He explained that Spaso House had been redecorated by a Soviet work crew without supervision by American security agents. The room was checked for bugs after the work was complete, but no listening devices were discovered. However, a second sweep was ordered when more modern detection technology was available. The hidden microphone was immediately discovered.

Kennan remembers the discovery this way: "Quivering with excitement, the technician extracted from the shattered

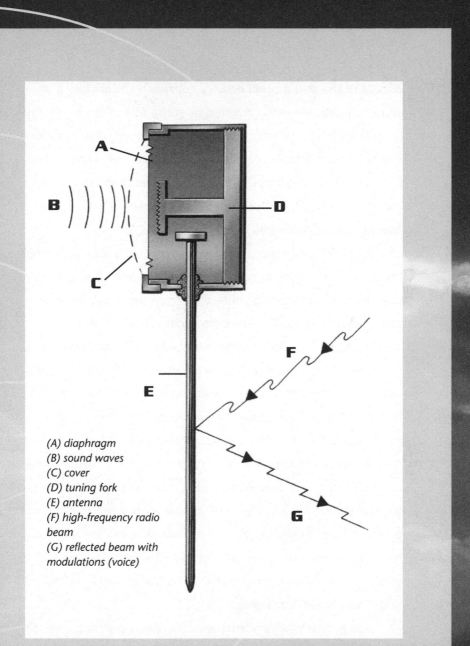

(A) diaphragm
(B) sound waves
(C) cover
(D) tuning fork
(E) antenna
(F) high-frequency radio beam
(G) reflected beam with modulations (voice)

The listening device found in the American embassy in Moscow

depths of the seal a small device, not much larger than a pen-cil . . . capable of being activated by some sort of electronic ray from outside the building. When not activated, it was almost impossible to detect." Although the device was crude when compared to today's eavesdropping devices, Kennan was cor-rect in assessing that the device "represented, for that day, a fantastically advanced bit of applied electronics."

To call the device electronic was not actually accurate, though, since it had no battery or power source. It was simply a resonator chamber with a flexible front wall that acted as a diaphragm. The sound waves from conversations in the room would vibrate this diaphragm. Meanwhile, Soviet agents in a truck outside the building would shoot a high-frequency radio beam, which would hit the bugging device's antenna. The mod-ulations from the device were reflected on the radio beam back to the truck, where they were interpreted as conversation.

When the United States displayed the bug, most experts in the intelligence community were confounded by it. How did the Thing—as it came to be called—work, since it had no power source? Peter Wright, the top spy scientist for England's MI5, answered that question and had MI5 technicians build a version of it (code-named Satyr), which was used by United States and British intelligence.

While many Americans were shocked by the Soviet's blatant eavesdropping, intelligence experts saw it for what it was, another example of a battle between two Cold War foes who were constantly trying to get the upper hand. In fact, the Spaso House had been under constant surveillance for decades. In the 1930s, guests at the U.S. ambassador's home were given cards welcoming them and warning them: *Every room is monitored by the KGB and all of the staff are employees of the KGB. We believe the garden also may be monitored. Your luggage may be searched two or three times a day. Nothing is ever stolen and they hardly disturb things.* So, the Thing surprised no seasoned intelligence officers.

And, as part of the Cold War cat-and-mouse game between the United States and the Soviet Union, the discovery of the listening device in the Great Seal was kept secret for eight years, until 1960, when the U.S. could use such information to its advantage. On May 26, 1960, U.S. Ambassador to the United Nations Henry Cabot Lodge, Jr., unveiled the "Great Seal Bug" before members of the UN Security Council to quiet Soviet accusations of U-2 spy flights. Lodge used the listening device to show the UN that the Soviets spied on Americans and thereby blunt a Soviet resolution denouncing the United States for its espionage flights.

Moles in Our House

Aldrich Ames

I n June 1957, after Aldrich Ames completed his sophomore year of high school, he took a summer job at the CIA head-quarters in nearby Langley, Virginia. He worked as a records analyst, marking classified documents for filing. He returned to the same job for the next two summers. Three years later, after he'd left college because of poor grades, Ames went back to work at the CIA, this time as a document analyst. So began the CIA career of Aldrich "Rick" Ames.

Ames's father had had a short (and unsuccessful) tenure as a CIA agent in Southeast Asia in the 1950s. Perhaps Aldrich Ames joined the CIA, in part, to carry on the work that his father had not done terribly well. He was accepted into the CIA's Career Trainee Program in 1967. As part of his training, he learned how to recruit and manage agents who were able and willing to provide actionable intelligence to the U.S. government. Agents who perform this sort of recruiting are called operations officers or case officers. Although Ames's psychological profile seemed to indicate that he was ill suited for such work—he did not have the easy, outgoing personality that such officers needed—he was considered a strong trainee. Finishing his training in October 1968, Ames received his first posting overseas in Ankara, Turkey.

In Ankara, Ames held the same job that he was to hold for most of his career: recruiting Russians or persons from other Communist countries. And, as was the case for most of his career, he wasn't successful or happy in that position. Some veteran agents didn't expect much from a first-year agent, but his supervisors were convinced he was not cut out for that job. One officer noted that Ames couldn't even succeed in the first level of the job, recruiting what are called access agents, people who did not themselves have intelligence but who have access to the people who did. Generally, a small stipend would be offered by an agent like Ames to secure the services of a secretary or low-level embassy official who worked for someone who would know valuable information.

Ames received strong ratings and was given a bump in grade and salary after the first year. That was the high point of his first assignment because his performance ratings declined over the next two years. His superiors felt that he was best suited to work behind a desk at Langley. Ames was crushed by the criticism of his work and considered leaving the agency. However, he decided to return to the job even though he would be stuck at headquarters. It was a decision that would start him on a path of treachery and betrayal.

Perhaps because he was better suited to handle paperwork rather than fieldwork, Ames received very good reviews from his superiors at Langley. But, more important, he worked in the Soviet–East European (SE) Division of the Directorate of Operations for four years. He specialized in clandestine operations. The United States remained locked in a cold war with the Soviet Union, so he received training in Russian and provided support for CIA operations against Russian officials. Before long, however, his ratings slipped as he began drinking alcohol heavily. Yet his drinking problem was never given the attention by his superiors that it deserved.

He next served in New York City from 1976 until 1981, but his performance continued to be inconsistent. Nonetheless, he received several promotions and a bonus, even though his inattention to detail became a more serious problem. For example, Ames left a briefcase filled with classified documents on a subway. The FBI was able to recover the briefcase, but they were unsure if the contents had been compromised while the briefcase was lost. In 1980, Ames left top-secret communications equipment unsecured in his office. Despite such serious breaches of security rules, he was never officially reprimanded.

Why would an intelligence agent who received lukewarm evaluations at best be allowed to continue in the service of his government in such a sensitive area, where he would have ready access to secret files? The most likely explanation seems to be the "good old boy" culture that can infect an agency like the CIA or the FBI. In such a male-dominated environment, the men who have worked there for a long time are protective of one another, and supervisors are often reluctant to discipline or fire agents whose performance does not meet the agency's standards.

The next stop for Ames was Mexico City, where he continued to concentrate on Soviet cases. At this point, his marriage was failing and his evaluations by his superiors were generally unenthusiastic. To make matters worse, Ames's drinking became a public problem, which should have been a red flag for his supervisors. An agent under the influence of liquor is a danger to the CIA and other agents since he may blurt out any of the secrets he knows. Instead, Ames was noted as a "social drinker," with "no serious alcohol problem."

Back at Langley in the fall of 1983, Ames was given the most unlikely of jobs when he was appointed counter-intelligence branch chief for Soviet operations, giving him access to the files of all CIA operations involving Russian intelligence officers worldwide. In addition, he had access to all CIA plans and operations against the KGB and its successor, the GRU. Rick Ames now had at his fingertips all the information that would make him dangerous to the CIA and its Soviet agents.

Ames's wife filed for divorce, and Ames agreed to pay her three hundred dollars a month for nearly four years. He also agreed to pay off more than thirty-three thousand dollars in credit-card debt. He later told an interviewer that he was "trying to make some money that I felt I needed very badly, and in a sense that I felt at the time, one of terrible desperation." It was at this point, the winter of 1984–1985, that he first considered the possibility of espionage as a means of easing his financial troubles.

In a sense, lax CIA oversight made it easy for him to follow through on his plan. He had been given approval to return to the field to cultivate Soviet officials in the hope of getting them to "turn" and agree to work for the CIA. Ames, of course, had a different reason for wanting to meet and cultivate Soviet officials. He got his chance when he met Sergei Dimitriyevich Chuvakhin, an arms control specialist in the Soviet Ministry of Foreign Affairs. Slowly the men began to understand each other. Chuvakhin understood that Ames was interested in trading intelligence for cash. Ames knew he had a deal.

On April 16, 1985, Rick Ames walked into the Soviet embassy in Washington, D.C., handed an envelope to the duty officer, and asked for Chuvakhin by name. After a short conversation with Chuvakhin, Ames walked out of the embassy, his first packet of secret intelligence delivered and received. He would make many more deliveries over the next nine years.

What was in that first envelope? A note detailing a few CIA cases involving Soviets who were working for the CIA. He also included one page from a CIA memo with his name highlighted, showing the KGB that he was in a position to offer them sensitive intelligence. Finally, he included a request for a payment of $50,000. Within a month, Ames received his first payment from the KGB. Knowing the value of this CIA mole, the KGB instructed Chuvakhin to ask Ames to continue their working relationship.

But Rick Ames's espionage did not stop with that one deal. In fact, before he was arrested, he met with Soviet handlers all over the world, depending on his posting, and delivered as many as one thousand pages a year. For one meeting with Chuvakhin in Washington, Ames walked out of CIA headquarters with five to seven pounds of secret message traffic in plastic bags. He knew that the CIA no longer inspected packages and briefcases carried out of the building by agency employees. On the evening in question, Ames calmly walked to his car in the parking lot, dumped the plastic bags in the trunk, and drove off to his meeting with Chuvakhin.

It didn't take the CIA very long to realize that something was dreadfully wrong with their Soviet operations. By the end of 1985, the CIA learned that three of its "assets" (useful agents for performing covert operations) had been arrested. Far more troubling, all had been executed. As one CIA officer put it, the KGB was "wrapping up our cases with reckless abandon." The agency found it odd, however, that the Soviets would "roll up," or shut down, the cases in such rapid succession by capturing and killing American agents, because such action could draw unwanted attention to anyone who had access to relevant information. Ames later said that the KGB had realized its mistake and took action from then on to be more careful with their roll-ups and do what it could to mislead the CIA. For example, they would set out bogus evidence that an operative had been discovered by other means, or they would simply let an agent continue his work, although under very strict surveillance, making sure that he was kept clear of sensitive information. In all, however, twenty cases had been compromised, causing a "virtual collapse" of the CIA's Soviet operations.

If the agency was quick to spot the problem, they were inexplicably slow in making a serious attempt to find the mole. Some CIA officers refused to face the possibility that there was a traitor in their ranks. In the meantime, Ames had remarried and was receiving large sums of money for his betrayal. One deposit made to a secret bank account was for $300,000. Each time he delivered intelligence to his handler, he received between $20,000 and $50,000. At the end of 1985, the Soviets informed Ames that they would pay him $2 million in addition to the money he had already received. The Soviets were eager to pay him.

Ames was making so much money that he didn't know what to do with it. In what ultimately led to his downfall, Ames spent a lot of it, telling people that his new wife's parents were very rich. He paid nearly half a million dollars cash for a home in an affluent Virginia suburb and then spent $100,000 for home improvements. He bought a white Jaguar sedan for $50,000, spent about $25,000 for his wife's graduate school program, and paid $14,300 for his son's nanny. And he did all this on an annual CIA salary that was not quite $70,000.

Ames needed a way to hide his illegal money. He deposited money in eight different U.S. banks and investment companies. He was careful with his deposits, making sure none was over $10,000, since banks need to report deposits over that level to a federal banking agency. He also opened bank accounts in Colombia and Italy, as well as in two Swiss banks: one in his name, the other in the name of his new mother-in-law. He listed himself as the primary trustee on the latter account, giving him quick access to the money. These accounts topped out at $1.8 million. It is estimated that from 1985 to 1993, Ames and his wife spent nearly $1.4 million (including on the house) and regularly racked up $50,000 on their credit cards.

Ames's extravagant spending did not go unnoticed by his colleagues at the CIA. One worker called his spending "blatantly excessive." This same coworker reported that Ames's spending was a common topic of office conversation. Another colleague knew that Ames's phone bill reached $5,000 per month. It was also common knowledge that Ames and his wife traveled frequently throughout Europe. Still, no one at Langley made the connection between Ames's sudden wealth and the disappearance of operatives in the Soviet Union.

Despite the danger flags that Rick Ames waved in its face, the CIA did nearly nothing to confront their agent or investigate his activities until 1986, when it established a special task force to look into the destruction of its Soviet program. In October of that year, the FBI learned that two of its Soviet operatives had been rolled up. The bureau responded with a task force team of its own. Despite a history of turf wars, the CIA and the FBI shared some intelligence with each other and finally agreed to an "off-site" conference to discuss the problem. But, as one CIA agent wrote, the agency made a "conscious decision . . . concerning the degree to which we are gong to cooperate with and open ourselves to the FBI."

While the CIA and FBI investigations were under way, Ames continued to spy. He did change his tactics, however, curtailing face-to-face meetings, relying, instead, on "signal sites" and "dead drops" to conduct his business. When Ames had documents to deliver to his handler, he would leave a mark at a signal site, often a simple chalk mark on a U.S. mailbox. The signal meant that his handlers could go to the dead drop that corresponded to that signal sight to pick up the documents. A dead drop is an out-of-the-way spot where documents and cash could be left, such as a drainage pipe ($30,000 in one-hundred-dollar bills is only about an inch and a quarter thick) in a secluded part of a park. When the Soviets had payment for the spy, they used the same signal site to let him know it could be retrieved at the dead drop. Their signal sites and dead drops were known by codes names, such as Smile and Hill (signal sites), and Bridge and Ground (dead drops).

The ongoing CIA–FBI investigation, begun in 1986, was marked by numerous dead ends and promising leads that turned out to disappoint the mole hunters. By the summer of 1987, the head of the CIA special task force was forced to concede that they needed to go "back to square one." The mole hunt was not renewed until 1991.

There does not seem to have been any one specific reason that the CIA wanted to reopen the case with the FBI. As one agent put it, the case was "always there and it was always an open wound that we wanted to solve."

By August, the CIA had identified 198 employees who had access to the pertinent documents. They flagged twenty-nine employees, including Ames, as priority targets. Ames's name rose to the top of each investigator's list, since, in addition to having access to files involved in the loss of agents, the investigators were not satisfied with the explanations for his sudden wealth. Ironically, though, Ames had passed a routine polygraph test earlier in the year. In November, the CIA/FBI unit interviewed Ames. Those involved in the interview came away feeling uneasy about Ames. They discovered that several meetings between Ames and Chuvakhin went unreported to his supervisors, a violation of CIA rules. With this new bit of information, the investigators decided it was time to intensify their scrutiny of Ames.

As they did, the evidence piled up, especially concerning his wealth. But the real breakthrough came when Sandy Grimes, an experienced officer in the Soviet Division of the CIA, compared the dates of the meetings between Ames and

Chuvakhin with the dates of his large bank deposits. She discovered that Ames made many of his cash deposits right after meetings with his handler. Next they discovered Ames's Swiss bank accounts. By October 1992 the joint unit was confident that Rick Ames was a Soviet mole. They gave him a code name: Nightmover.

The FBI began a closer investigation of Ames, initiating electronic surveillance of his home and office. They installed a tracking device on his car. When they searched his office at Langley, they discovered 144 documents that were not related to his CIA assignments. In June the FBI tapped the phones in Ames's house. Two months later they decided to launch a "trash cover" of the home. They didn't need a search warrant to search his garbage because it was outside the home and considered fair game. The plan called for a CIA van to cruise slowly by the Ames's house in the dark of night, while agents dragged his trash can into the van and quickly replaced it with an identical can. Although some of the agents were worried that Ames may have sensed that the investigation was focusing on him, the Bureau carried out its operation. It paid immediate dividends when they found a crumpled sticky note.

According to an FBI "translation," this message, which was determined to be in Ames's handwriting, said that Ames was ready to meet his handler in Bogotá, Colombia, on

I AM READY TO MEET
AT B ON 1 OCT.
    I CANNOT READ
NORTH 13-19 SEPT.
    IF YOU WILL
MEET AT B ON 1 OCT.
PLS SIGNAL NORTH u
OF 20 SEPT TO CONF.
NO MESSAGE AT PIPE.
    IF YOU CANNOT MEE.
1 OCT, SIGNAL NORTH AFTER
27 SEPT WITH MESSAGE AT
    PIPE.

An incriminating note written by Ames and discovered by the FBI in a search of his trash

October 1. He would be away on CIA business on September 13 to 19, so he would not be able to pick up any messages. He asked the KGB to leave a signal at North (a telephone pole) or to leave a message at the dead drop Pipe if the meeting was canceled.

The damning evidence in this note was enough to allow the FBI to move to the next level of surveillance. When Ames and his family left for a family vacation on October 9, 1993, the FBI moved into the home and conducted a thorough search. As one agent said, "The best stuff we got was from the hard drive of his computer." All pertinent information was downloaded and copied to floppy disks. Although the phones in the house had been tapped since midsummer, the FBI now planted listening devices throughout the house. In a few hours, the FBI team was gone.

With Ames's phones tapped and his house bugged, there was little he or his family could say or do that would escape notice by the FBI. The evidence against Ames grew. Still, the FBI hoped for more and kept Ames under constant physical surveillance. However, in early 1994, the FBI received word that the CIA was sending Ames to Moscow to participate in a conference on drug trafficking. Knowing that they could not postpone his trip without rousing Ames's suspicions and fearful that the mole might defect once he was on Soviet soil, the FBI decided that it was time to arrest Rick Ames.

On February 21, 1994, Ames left his family at home while he drove to his office to get a few things he needed for his trip to Russia the next day. On a one-way street about a block and a half from his home, he pulled his new red Jaguar behind a car stopped at the stop sign. The car next to that one was ready to turn left. But, for some reason, neither moved. Before Ames could figure out why, he saw cars with red lights flashing pull up behind him. Two men in suits stepped out of one of the cars and approached Ames. The spy rolled down his window and both men flashed their picture identity cards. "FBI," one of them called. "You're under arrest. Get out of the car." Ames stepped out of his car. He was turned around and handcuffed. The arrest of Aldrich Ames took less than sixty seconds.

What motivated this career CIA agent to become a mole for the Soviet Union? In interviews after his arrest, Ames claimed that he considered this first exchange with the Soviets to be a one-time deal. He did it for the money. He called it "running my little scam," in which he would give the Soviets the names of agents and their cash would solve his financial difficulties. He also rationalized his betrayal by saying that he was really giving the KGB names that they already knew, since they were Soviet agents that the CIA had turned. In Ames's mind, the KGB already knew that the agents were spying for Russia. They just didn't know that they were now double agents. Ames was eager to sell this information to the KGB.

The case of Aldrich Ames pointed out many defects in the operations of the CIA. By the time Congressional hearings were over and Ames was locked away for life with no chance

Aldrich Ames, CIA mole, is arrested not far from his home.

for parole, R. James Woosley Jr., the director of the CIA, had resigned. Congress demanded that the agency clean house and revamp procedures to ensure that the likes of Ames could not penetrate the CIA again. No one knew at that time, but the FBI, instrumental in tracking down the CIA mole, would soon need to investigate a mole of its own.

Cyber Espionage

It SEEMS THAT A WEEK doesn't go by without news about computer hackers stealing massive amounts of information from supposedly secure databases. We read stories of computer viruses, worms, and Trojan horses that affect millions of computer users. Computers have become another target for thieves and spies who are looking for information that will give them or their employers valuable intelligence. It should come as no surprise that cyber espionage has grown right along with the popularity and sophistication of computers. With some elementary software and a few clicks of a mouse, spies can sit in front of their computers and spy on computers thousands of miles away. The GhostNet episode serves as a cautionary tale of cyber espionage.

In the spring of 2008, members of the Dalai Lama's government-in-exile in three locations in Dharamsala, India, had reason to believe that their computers had been compromised. They asked the Information Warfare Monitor (IWM) to investigate. IWM includes researchers from the Munk Centre for International Studies at the University of Toronto. Collaborating in the investigation were researchers from Cambridge University, in the U.K., and Dartmouth College.

An exhaustive ten-month investigation revealed shocking information about GhostNet, the name given to the huge cyber spying operation. The researchers discovered a network of nearly 1,300 infected host computers in 103 countries. Nearly 30 percent of the infected computers were considered high-value targets, such as computers in ministries of foreign affairs, embassies, international organizations, and new media outlets. The targeted computers were spread throughout the world, in places like Iran, Brussels, South Korea, Portugal, and Pakistan. The investigators found interfaces that allowed the spy (or spies) to send instructions to, and receive data from, compromised computers.

How was such a spy system possible? It all started when a Trojan horse, a hidden computer virus, known as ghOstRAT was sent to the computers at the Dalai Lama's headquarters as an attachment in a legitimate-sounding e-mail. When the attachment was opened, ghOstRAT spread throughout the computer, including any e-mail address book, which allowed the Trojan horse to be sent to still more computers. In computer language, *RAT* means Remote Access Trojan and gives the hacker a back door to the infected computer, allowing it to do all sorts of malicious things.

ghOstRAT attached itself to interesting files and information. It kept track of keystrokes, recording whatever the users typed. It could even turn on a webcam and take a picture of the persons using the computer, and turn on the microphone to record conversations! Cyber spies could use GhostNet to gather files and e-mail contact information, lists of meetings and the names of who attended, organizational budgets, and lists of visitors. In other words, it was an espionage gold mine. What made this particular case of cyber espionage so difficult to combat was that the malware was disguised in the emails, which made it difficult for commercial anti-virus programs to detect the problem. In fact, only about a third of the thirty-four anti-virus programs used to detect such hacking could find the malware hidden in the document.

As one computer expert put it, while the tools used to breach the Dalai Lama's walls were "relatively simple, the social engineering bit is quite meticulous." In other words, the hackers studied the types of e-mails and documents that the government-in-exile received, then took pains to create bogus e-mails and attachments that appeared to be real. When opened, the documents looked and sounded real, but they contained a hidden code that would download and install software that would serve the spies.

The investigation discovered that all the information gathered in GhostNet was sent to remote servers in China, although IWM stopped short of accusing the Chinese government of masterminding GhostNet. However, researchers at Cambridge

University who focused on the computers at the Office of His Holiness the Dalai Lama "dubs the spy network 'snooping dragon'" and indicates that Chinese government and intelligence services are the masterminds behind the hacking.

Other researchers believed that, while the hacking may have been done by private citizens in China, it seemed unlikely that it could have been carried out without the knowledge (and possibly approval) of the Chinese government. The Chinese embassy in London denied having anything to do with Ghost-Net, calling the investigation and its findings "a propaganda campaign." The Chinese consulate in New York called any suggestion of China's involvement "nonsense." Nonetheless, within a day after China denied any complicity in GhostNet, the servers that had been gathering intelligence went offline.

Robert Hanssen

Robert Hanssen's life path took many twists and turns before he settled on a career in the FBI. He grew up in Chicago in the 1950s, the son of an emotionally abusive and demeaning father. Hanssen spent his life trying to measure up to his father's expectations. A bright student who excelled in science, Hanssen lacked the social skills of his friends and was uncomfortable with other people. Yet underneath his awkward exterior was a risk taker. He enjoyed the rush he got from pushing the limits, such as by driving his car as fast as he could before slamming on the brakes and sending the car into a crazy spin, often to the terror of the friends riding with him.

After college, Hanssen worked as an accountant for Sears, but he soon quit when he found the work unbearably boring. He decided to become a Chicago police officer, like his father. Hanssen worked in the early 1970s as a member of C5, the internal affairs unit, whose job was investigating other cops. When he found the job unsatisfying, he applied to work for the FBI. He was rejected the first time he applied because of bad eyesight, but he was accepted on his second try. On January 12, 1976, Robert Hanssen began his training at the FBI Academy at Quantico, Virginia.

Hanssen served his first two years with the FBI as a field agent in Indiana but was transferred to the New York City office in 1978. Despite the excitement of working in such a dynamic international city, Hanssen began to become disillusioned with the bureaucracy of the FBI. He hadn't worked for the Bureau very long before his arrogance began to show itself. Hanssen considered most of the other agents, as well as his supervisors, to be his intellectual inferiors.

One evening in 1980, Hanssen's wife, Bonnie, returned home unexpectedly from errands and found her husband trying to cover up a pile of cash. She was dumbfounded. Hanssen told her part of the truth, that he had received the money from Soviet military intelligence officers for useless information that he had passed on to them. The truth was

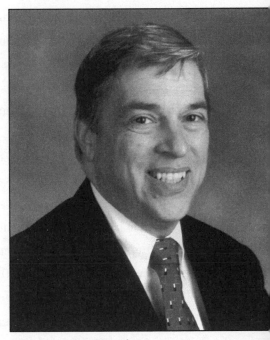

Robert Hanssen, FBI mole

grimmer than Hanssen's fiction. He had turned over to the Soviets the identity of Dmitri Polyakov, a Soviet general who had been a mole for the FBI for more than two decades, operating under the code name Tophat. Hanssen's "useless" information led to Polyakov's execution by the Soviets.

Believing her husband's lie, Bonnie was still horrified that her deeply religious husband would have any dealings with the Communists, even if he had duped them. She didn't know what to do. She finally decided that he needed to seek help from the parish priest. Reluctantly, Hanssen did so. He then apologized deeply to Bonnie, begging her to forgive him. She did, believing that his dealings with the Communists were behind him. Little did she know that they were just beginning.

As the next few years passed, Hanssen became even more disillusioned with the Bureau, feeling more like an outsider then ever before. When he was transferred to the Budget Unit, his disgust for the bureaucracy and its old-fashioned methods grew. He frequently mocked the seriously outdated computer system. He had contempt for the Bureau's leaders, fantasizing about the "bold, brave FBI agent in the dark suit," acting on the orders of J. Edgar Hoover, the FBI's legendary director.

Robert Hanssen did little to become a more likable or approachable fellow, and his social skills had not improved much from his high-school days. He rarely participated in conversations. Other agents made fun of him, calling him the Mortician or Dr. Death because he always wore dark suits. Agents remembered him as "an oddball out" and "very dour." He had "fairly long, canine teeth that would give him a vampire-like appearance." And, as one of his administrators said, he was "one of the smartest FBI agents I ever met."

Grateful that his wife had accepted his apology, Hanssen had a second chance to spy. He realized that he needed to operate much more carefully. He still felt the sting of the embarrassment of getting caught and vowed that it would never happen again. He decided to work for the KGB and do whatever he needed to do to protect himself from discovery. Even as he mapped out his safeguards, Hanssen convinced himself that he could live the fantasy life of a spy who would prove himself to be smarter than the FBI *and* the KGB.

Hanssen made his initial contact with Victor Ivanovich Cherkashin, the number-two KGB agent in Washington. Although Hanssen had no way of knowing it, Cherkashin was also Aldrich Ames's handler. Hanssen wrote a letter to Cherkashin, but, true to his promise to himself, he was very careful with the first step in his new double life. First of all, he mailed the letter from a Maryland suburb of Washington, D.C., rather than from New York, where he was then posted. He had been in the capital on Bureau business, so it was easy for him to drive over to Maryland and mail the letter, which he hadn't signed. Hanssen made sure that the letter and its envelope bore no marks that would tip off the Bureau agents, who were always watching Cherkashin. To add another layer of protection, he addressed the letter to the home of Victor M. Degtyar, another KGB agent. Inside that envelope was a second envelope with the name of Victor Cherkashin on it as well as a clear warning: DO NOT OPEN. TAKE THIS ENVELOPE UNOPENED TO VICTOR I. CHERKASHIN. And it was in *that* envelope that Hanssen divulged information that he hoped would establish him as an inside player with formidable sources. Hanssen included:

- The names of three KGB double agents (All three were recalled to Moscow. Two were executed, while the third was banished to a labor camp for fifteen years.)
- Information about a top-secret information collection operation
- News of the Bureau's electronic eavesdropping operation targeting Soviet communications

So it was that Robert Hanssen took a big step on the road of betrayal.

After considering the methods of delivery of information, Hanssen developed a system of signal sites and dead drops that prevented face-to-face meetings between him and his handler. For example, Hanssen marked a mailbox on a street corner not far from his home with a small piece of masking tape or a short line drawn with a piece of chalk to let his handler know that there was a package waiting for him. Hanssen's handler watched for the mark then furtively removed it and went to the dead drop to pick up a bundle of secret documents. Hanssen had developed about a dozen dead drops, each code-named, including

In a dead drop code-named Ellis, Hanssen hid secret documents under this bridge.

Bob, Charlie, Doris, Ellis, and Grace. One of his favorite dead drops was Ellis, a footbridge in a park not far from his home.

When Hanssen did have written communication with his handler, he encoded times and dates with what is called the "minus 6" formula. Here's an example of a passage that Hanssen included at the end of one of his letters:

> *If you wish to continue our discussions, please have someone run an advertisement in the Washington Times during the week of 1/12/87 or 1/19/87, for sale, "Dodge Diplomat, 1971, needs engine work, $1000." Give a phone number and time-of-day in the advertisement where I can call.*

Although the ad sounds legitimate, when the "minus 6" formula is applied to the dates—subtracting 6 from the month and day—his handler knew that the ad needed to appear the week of July 6, 1986, or July 13, 1986.

Carefully constructing a series of twists and turns to keep his identity a secret, Hanssen successfully avoided discovery. However, part of the credit for his longevity as a mole must be given to the inept actions of the FBI. Like the CIA in the Ames case, the Bureau would not believe that the mole was one of their own. Yet they missed a golden opportunity to catch Hanssen in 1990, after his wife had caught him with the pile of money. Bonnie Hanssen told her brother, Mark Wauck, an FBI special agent in Chicago, about what she had seen. When Wauck heard about the cash his brother-in-law had tried to conceal, the agent went to his supervisor and told him what Hanssen had been up to. He also reported how his brother-in-law was spending far too much money for an FBI agent. He concluded his meeting by saying that he believed Robert Hanssen was spying for the Soviet Union. His superiors did nothing. Wauck was furious.

Why didn't the FBI initiate an investigation of Wauck's allegations? There are theories, but no certainty about the reason. Was the Bureau simply protecting one of its own? Did Wauck's information simply disappear in the bureaucracy of the FBI? Wauck wondered if a friend of Hanssen's stopped an investigation, but given Hanssen's relationship with his colleagues, this seemed unlikely. Agent Wauck told his story at a time when global politics were changing. The Berlin Wall had been torn down. The Soviet Union had collapsed, leading to closer ties between the intelligence agencies of the two superpowers. Is it possible that the investigation of Hanssen at that point was buried for fear of creating an embarrassment to East and West?

Regardless of the reason, Hanssen was not investigated in 1990, and his work as a mole continued into 1991. Then he suddenly dropped out of the spy game and didn't resume his role for eight years, although he continued to work for the FBI. With a new, more open regime in Russia, it became riskier to spy for the KGB since it thrived in a totalitarian state. Hanssen sat on the sidelines with a keen eye trained on the political situation in Russia.

Finally, in 2000 his attitude changed with the political changes in Russia. The reformers were struggling in their attempt to bring Russia into the modern political world. Boris Yeltsin was out as president, and Vladimir Putin, a former KGB spy, assumed the role. With Putin in power, Russia reverted in many ways to the authoritarian ways of the past, meaning more secrets, more centralized control. Hanssen knew it was his time to return to his world of dark secrets.

It's ironic that the more successful he became as a spy, the greater were his chances of being uncovered. As David Major, one of Hanssen's only Bureau friends, put it, "He forgot that the better he was, the more at risk he was." In other words, as Hanssen delivered thousands of pages of classified documents to the KGB, he built a thick case file. And the thicker it became, the more ripples it made with the FBI, giving the Bureau more sources to pinpoint him as the mole. One historian observed that as Hanssen's case file grew, it became "a valuable bargaining chip for a Russian mole doing business with the CIA." So, despite how careful Robert Hanssen had been, his "success" ultimately brought him down.

On the afternoon of February 2, 2001, FBI Director Louis Freeh reported to Attorney General John Ashcroft that the Bureau had received a case file from Russia detailing a staggering security breech. The file contained thousands of pages of sensitive intelligence and secret documents, and the paper trail went back sixteen years. With the betrayal of Rick Ames still in their minds, the FBI believed that the mole was a CIA operative, perhaps someone who had worked with Ames or who had taken over when Ames was arrested. However, one bit of evidence in the case file told a different story: fingerprints on a black plastic trash bag, used by the mole to protect documents he left at a dead drop. Careful analysis of the fingerprints indicated that they belonged to Special Agent Robert Hanssen.

There was more corroborating evidence on a tape recording of a brief telephone conversation between the mole and a known KGB operative. A number of Bureau agents listened to the original version of the recording as well as a version that had been electronically "cleaned" of background noise. Two agents who had worked with Hanssen had no doubt that the voice of the mole belonged to "the Mortician."

With this evidence, the investigation of Robert Hanssen kicked into high gear. Armed with the proper legal paperwork, the FBI bugged Hanssen's office, home, and car. FBI agents discovered that Hanssen had made extensive use of its Electronic Case File (ECF), a computer database that tracked all ongoing investigation. From the summer of 1997 until the end of 2000, Hanssen had searched the ECF for his name, the name of his street, and the term *dead drop* nearly eighty times. The bureau that Hanssen had always found intellectually inferior to him had outsmarted him by not entering the details of their investigation of Hanssen into the database.

The evidence against Hanssen mounted. When agents searched the trunk of his car, they discovered a roll of white athletic tape and a box of colored chalk, both used at his signal sites. They also found seven classified documents from Bureau files. In addition, they found a roll of wide, clear shipping tape and a number of black plastic trash bags. The agents photographed the objects rather than taking them, careful not to alert Hanssen to the investigation.

Details that would be considered circumstantial evidence filled in some of the blanks for the investigators:

- Two of the dead drops most frequently used by Hanssen were close to two houses that he had lived in. One dead drop, in fact, was only about sixty steps from his home.
- Although Hanssen thought he had outwitted the Bureau when he mailed his first letter to the KGB from Maryland instead of from New York City,

investigators soon discovered that the letter was postmarked during a time when Hanssen was in Washington on Bureau business.

- Hanssen's PDA made mention of the Ellis dead drop.
- And perhaps the most telling bit of circumstantial evidence was the fact that various positions that Hanssen held with the FBI over the years gave him access to the very information that had been passed on to the Soviets.

For his part, Robert Hanssen seemed to sense that he was in the endgame of his work for the KGB. After attending church on Sunday, February 18, Hanssen prepared his final package of intelligence, which included a stack of documents as well as a computer diskette. He also included a note to his handler. "Dear Friends," the letter began. "I thank you for your assistance these many years. It seems, however, that my greatest utility to you has come to an end, and it is time to seclude myself from active service." He went on to tell his handler that he'd been promoted to a "higher do-nothing Senior Executive job outside of regular access to information within the counterintelligence program."

After dropping off a friend at Dulles International Airport, Hanssen drove to Foxstone Park, where he carefully placed a piece of white tape on a pole on the park's entrance sign.

This was the signal to his handlers that he would be leaving a package at the Ellis dead drop. After carefully hiding his bundle, he turned to walk back down the path to his car. He didn't make it. He was surrounded by fellow FBI agents, all with weapons drawn and pointed at him.

Hanssen was neither surprised nor impressed that the agents had finally discovered his secret. In fact, his words were filled with arrogant disdain. "What took you so long?" he asked as he was handcuffed and led to an FBI car. In the months to come, that question would linger in the mind of many people in the intelligence community.

Robert Hanssen's spy case ended the same way Rick Ames's case did, with a guilty plea and the realization that he would spend the rest of his life in a federal prison. He was saved from the death penalty when he agreed to answer truthfully any questions put to him in the FBI debriefing sessions. He further agreed to take a lie detector test, ironically, something he had not been required to do in his twenty-five years with the Bureau. Finally, Hanssen accepted a condition that denied him access to a computer for as long as he lived.

Despite his dire situation, Hanssen continued to defy the Bureau, and it nearly led to the revocation of his plea agreement. He failed one lie detector test, and debriefing team agents reported that Hanssen's "cooperation concerning his finances, the significance of his espionage, and his motives were problematic." Despite these reservations, the judge who reviewed the record saw no reason to revoke Hanssen's plea bargain.

The list of documents, operations, and double agents that Robert Hanssen handed over to the Soviets is staggering: over 6,000 pages of documents and nearly thirty computer diskettes. William Webster, former FBI director, said Hanssen's treason was like a "five-hundred-year flood." Because of Hanssen, the FBI changed the way it monitors its agents, much like the way the CIA made changes to prevent a repeat of the Ames debacle. Nonetheless, perhaps we should bear in mind the words of Robert Hanssen's attorney, who said that his client was "as artful a spy as we've ever seen. Except for the one who's out there now and hasn't been caught."

Spy Satellites

EVEN BEFORE THE U-2 SPY PLANE piloted by Francis Gary Powers was shot down over the Soviet Union in 1960, the United States was hard at work developing the next generation of spies in the sky, the reconnaissance satellites. In 1959, two years after the Russians launched Sputnik, the U.S. launched the Corona satellite, the first man-made object to be put into orbit. The Corona satellite was the first of the U.S. satellites designed to take photographs from space. It is estimated that between 1959 and 1972, the Corona was launched more than one hundred times. U.S. intelligence services constantly made changes to the Corona, modernizing the launch vehicle as well as the camera.

The Corona was the first in the KH, or "keyhole" line of satellites. It was equipped with a single camera that took panoramic black-and-white photographs. The resolution of such early satellite cameras was about six feet, meaning that the camera could photograph structures and landscape features of that size or larger.

One of the most important parts of the spy satellite is the camera. As with other spy technology, the orbiting camera system has been constantly improved. One major improvement in the first few years of Corona development was the addition of a second camera. The two cameras photographed 30 degrees apart, one camera pointing forward, one pointing backward. The satellites gathered evidence on how fast the USSR was producing long-range bombers and ballistic missiles.

The Corona spy satellite

Even though the technology was constantly changing, the method of recovering the film was primitive. Used film canisters returned to earth in a capsule, or "bucket," for analysis. The bucket fell to earth attached to a parachute and was then plucked from the air by specially equipped airplanes. The bucket was also designed to float so it could be retrieved from the ocean by boat if the recovery plane missed the parachute. Now, of course, photographic intelligence is electronically relayed to earth.

Since the days of the early keyhole satellites, satellite and optic technology have improved dramatically and their uses now go beyond the military. They deliver television signals, weather reports, and telephone calls. Every Global Positioning System (GPS) device relies on signals sent from satellites. Search and rescue teams use satellites to receive emergency signals from ships in distress.

In addition, satellites provide invaluable information to the military. Satellites orbiting the earth relay encoded messages, eavesdrop on radio signals, notify our military of enemy troop movements, and monitor nuclear testing. Cameras in modern satellites have a much sharper resolution than the Corona-era cameras. Intelligence experts agree that the current breed of satellites is capable of taking pictures with a clarity that was unimagined when the Corona was launched.

Beyond such traditional military uses, satellites have been used more extensively since the attack on the World Trade Center and the Pentagon on September 11, 2001. Although shrouded in secrecy, details of the Echelon satellite system have emerged and are controversial. The Echelon satellites are developed and launched by the National Reconnaissance Office (NRO), an agency that was not officially acknowledged until the 1990s. The NRO operates all the spy satellites used by various U.S. intelligence agencies for taking pictures and eavesdropping on communication transmissions, including e-mails. Although U.S. intelligence officials maintain that none of the satellites is used for commercial espionage, many countries are skeptical about such reassurances. In addition to the Echelon satellites, the National Security Agency has its own group of eavesdropping satellites, code-named Groundbreaker. Satellites of these agencies orbit several thousand miles above the earth, deploying antennas the size of football fields. These antennas can listen in on ground-line conversations all over the world.

As amazing as these intelligence gathering advances may sound, it is clear that the technology and capabilities of spy satellites will continue to develop into the twenty-first century.

Source Notes

Chapter 1: Outspying the British

p. 6: "Washington did not . . . outspied us!": Allen, p. 149.

p. 8: "Health and Spirits of the Army, Navy, and City": Allen, p. 51.

p. 9: "I live in daily fear . . . unmanned me": Rose, p. 258.

p. 9–10: "faithful friend . . . in all respects": Ford, p. 165.

p. 14: "Every 356 . . . outwit them all": Ford, pp. 198–199.

p. 14: "Did her social position . . . his aide?": Ford, p. 207.

p. 17: "355 remains . . . without a name": Ford, p. 321.

p. 18: "In a Word, Sir, we must have it": Robert Morris, *The Papers of Robert Morris, vol. 6, 1781–1874* (Pittsburgh: University of Pittsburgh Press, 1984), p. 450.

p. 20: "a crippled man": Walter Isaacson, *Benjamin Franklin: An American Life* (New York: Simon and Schuster, 2003), p. 340.

p. 20: "blood money," and "sold": P. K. Rose, "The Founding Fathers of American Intelligence" (Washington, DC: Center for the Study of Intelligence, 2009). https://www.cia.gov/library/center-for-the-study-of-intelligence/csi-publications/books-and-monographs/the-founding-fathers-of-american-intelligence/art-1.htm.

p. 27: "undertake the part in question" and "small sum of ready money": Randall, pp. 502 and 503.

p. 27: "a drawing of the works . . . engineer" and "might take . . . loss": Randall, p. 507.

p. 28: "key to America" and "proceed to West Point . . . dependencies": Randall, pp. 513 and 517.

p. 29: "mysteriously": Randall, p. 532.

p. 30: "[Major André] was so fully convinced . . . to your Excellency": Randall, p. 546.

p. 34: "Gentlemen, I hope . . . party?": Randall, p. 553.

p. 36: Washington's instructions for writing with invisible ink: Allen, pp. 69–70.

Chapter 2: Spies in Blue and Gray

p. 46: "Slave power . . . despotic": Varon, pp. 48–49.

p. 46: "profoundly betrayed": Varon, p. 35.

p. 47: "alone went . . . in blue": Varon, p. 85.

p. 49: "correspondent in Richmond": Varon, p. 111.

p. 50: "write me of course . . . at the North": Varon, pp. 111–112.

p. 56: "narrow and loathsome," "nearly to death," and "Great Yankee Wonder": Varon, p. 125.

p. 57: "She risked everything . . . Union preserved": Varon, p. 252.

p. 66: "irresistible": Blackman, p. 7.

p. 68: "We rely upon you . . . a debt": Blackman, p. 45.

p. 69: "agent of Rose's undoing": Blackman, p. 49.

p. 70: "vocabulary of colour": Blackman, p. 94.

p. 70: "as being equal to those of their best engineers" and *"as well they might"*: Blackman, p. 92.

p. 72: "made my heart leap with joy": Blackman, p. 236.

p. 76: "Black Dispatches" and "If I want to find out . . . all I want": Markle, p. 62.

Chapter 3: Espionage Comes of Age in World War I

p. 80: "Certainly . . . not his business": Richelson, p. 5.

p. 90: "How Germany Has Worked . . . Agent's Letters": *New York World,* August 15, 1915.

p. 90: "merely a storm in a tea-cup": Jonathan Heinrich Bernstroff, *My Three Years in America* (New York: Scribner's, 1920), p. 197.

p. 90: "huge and expensive" and "made to backfire, dealing a devastating blow": O'Toole, p. 225.

p. 90: "Our contracts . . . came to an end": Franz von Papen, *Memoirs* (New York: Dutton, 1953), p. 44.

p. 91: "hiring destructive . . . organizations," "destruction agents," "mobilize immediately," and "where munitions are being loaded . . . and Russia": Witcover, p. 65.

p. 93: "I'll buy up what I can and blow up what I can't": Witcover, p. 84.

p. 96: "11 [railroad cars] . . . explosives" and "ten barges . . . explosives," and "The fire had started . . . for us to do anything": James M. Powles, "Terror Strikes Black Tom Island," *American History,* October 2004, p. 30.

p. 99: 5.0 on the Richter scale: Liberty State Park. http://www.state.nj.us/dep/ parksandforests/parks/liberty_state_park/liberty_blacktomexplosion.html.

p. 99: registered a 2.3: Lamont-Doherty Seismographic Network. http:// www.ldeo.columbia.edu/LCSN/Eq/20010911_WTCC/WTC_LDEO_KIM.pdf.

p. 99: "mentally deficient Hungarian immigrant": Witcover, p. 166.

p. 100: "intricate, affectionate . . . in elegant style": Denise Noe, "Mata Hari," TruTV.com. http://www.truetv.com/library/crime/terrorists_spies/ spies/hari/1.html.

p. 102: "You have made me suffer . . . and end to this": Toni Bentley, *Sisters of Salome* (New Haven: Yale University Press, 2002), pp. 116–117; Julie Wheelwright, *The Fatal Lover: Mata Hari and the Myth of Women in Espionage* (London: Collins & Brown, 1992), p. 74.

p. 103: "spy academy" and "codes, ciphers . . . enemy arms": Erika Ostrovsky, *Eye of Dawn: The Rise and Fall of Mata Hari* (New York: Macmillan, 1978), pp. 128–129.

p. 103: "little mysteries of counterespionage" and "professional secrecy": Magaret H. Darrow, *French Women and the First World War* (New York: Berg, 2000), p. 294.

p. 106: "reading Berlin's messages . . . the German recipients": Tuchman, p. 14.

p. 106: "ingenuity . . . inspired guessing": Tuchman, p. 14.

p. 112: "England to make . . . few months" and "lost territories . . . Arizona": Tuchman, p. 146.

p. 114: "arranges the conditions . . . for your Excellency": Tuchman, p. 102.

p. 116: "Never before or since . . . secret message": Kahn, p. 297.

p. 121: "were completely confused . . . their wiretaps": Kenny A. Franks, *Citizen Soldiers* (Norman: University of Oklahoma Press, 1984), p. 30.

Chapter 4: Espionage Gets Organized in World War II

p. 125: "collect and analyze . . . available to the government": Central Intelligence Agency, "The Office of Strategic Services: America's First Intelligence Agency" (Washington, D.C.: Center for the Study of Intelligence, 2000). https://www.cia.gov/library/center-for-the-study-of-intelligence/csi-publications/books-and-monographs/oss/art02.htm.

p. 128: "The woman who limps . . . destroy her": McIntosh, p. 114.

p. 130–131: Virginia Hall's contacts: Binney, pp. 124–125.

p. 131: "would give anything . . . bitch": Binney, p. 123.

p. 132: Cuthbert story: Binney, p. 123; McIntosh, p. 118. "God knows . . . the mountains": Binney, p. 123.

p. 132: "briefing officer for the boys": Binney, p. 129.

p. 133: "I found a few . . . eager to help": Binney, p. 131.

p. 135: "still operational . . . to get busy": McIntosh, p. 125. "thousands of bulbs": Binney, p. 138; McIntosh, p. 127.

p. 139: smallest commercial camera: *The Guinness Book of Records* (New York: Facts on File, 1995), p. 158.

p. 140: "the greatest . . . World War II": Haufler, p. 78.

p. 141: "rabid Nazi supporter" and "I began to use . . . staunch Nazi": Haufler, p. 80.

p. 143: "fifteen ships . . . Lisbon": Haufler, p. 82.

p. 145: "He came to us as . . . he had already set up": Haufler, p. 83.

p. 146: "Gerbers . . . flowers please": Pujol and West, p. 142.

p. 149: "Harris and Garbo . . . times of their lives": Holt, p. 212.

p. 150: "Gutter Fighting," "You're interested only . . . or be killed," and "a silent, deadly . . . quickly": O'Donnell, pp. 4 and 5.

p. 152: "He wined and dined . . . and dined him," "We were simply to come . . . they didn't know us," and "With any lie . . . truth as possible": O'Donnell, pp. 10 and 11.

p. 153: "surely there's no harm," "notebooks full of information," and "Just being a nice guy . . . areas": O'Donnell, p. 12.

Chapter 5: Cold War Spies

p. 158: dig a hole and bury it: Stafford, p. 79.

p. 163: a stack 10 feet wide, 15 feet deep, and 8 feet high: Stafford, p. 120.

p. 164: "Most intelligence ... project starts": Dulles, *The Craft of Naval Intelligence*.

p. 165: "We've got a problem": Stafford, p. 148.

p. 166: "It's gone": Stafford, p. 153.

p. 167: "I handed to him . . . previous day": Huntington.

p. 167: "asked me to meet . . . fresh developments": Huntington.

p. 168: "a bonanza to Western counterintelligence specialists": Stafford, p. 138.

p. 168: "Whether it was sexy . . . doubt it": Huntington.

p. 168–169: "The evidence suggests . . . to go to war": Weiner, p. 129.

p. 171: "very close approximation . . . were faced with" and "Text of message . . . Signature of message": Wright, pp. 233 and 232.

p. 174: "the enemy will have . . . technologies," "Our intelligence tells us essentially nothing," and "another Pearl Harbor," and "an extraordinary absence of knowledge": Taubman, p. 24.

p. 175: "was just appalling": William J. Broad, "Spy Satellites' Early Role as 'Floodlight' Coming Clear,' New York Times, September 12, 1995, C-10.

p. 177: adapted from sailplane designs: Pedlow and Welzenbach, p. 47.

p. 182: "would be impossible . . . equipment intact": Ambrose, p. 279.

p. 183: "no idea . . . orange-colored light": Nash, p. 395.

p. 185: "I must tell you . . . have said": H. Hanak, Soviet Foreign Policy Since the Death of Stalin (New York: Routledge, 1972), p. 115.

p. 185: "there was no authorization for any such flight": Ambrose, p. 286.

p. 188, 190: "Quivering with excitement . . . to detect" and "represented . . . electronics": George F. Kennan, Memoirs, vol. 2: 1950–1963 (Boston: Little, Brown, 1972), pp. 155 and 156.

p. 191: "Every room is . . . disturb things.": http://www.spybusters.com/ Great_Seal_Bug.html

Chapter 6: Moles in Our House

p. 197: "social drinker" and "no serious alcohol problem": Senate Select Committee.

p. 197: "trying to make . . . desperation": National Security Archives interview with Aldrich Ames. http://www.gwu.edu/~nsarchiv/coldwar/ interviews/episode21/aldrich1.html.

p. 199: "wrapping up our cases with reckless abandon": Senate Select Committee.

p. 200: "virtual collapse": Senate Select Committee.

p. 201: "blatantly excessive": Senate Select Committee.

p. 202: "conscious decision . . . to the FBI": Wise, p. 180.

p. 203: "back to square one" and "always there . . . wanted to solve": Senate Select Committee.

p. 205: "I am ready . . . message at pipe": Senate Select Committee.

p. 206: "The best stuff . . . his computer": Wise, p. 237.

p. 207: "FBI . . . the car": Wise, p. 2.

p. 207: "running my little scam": National Security Archives interview with Aldrich Ames. http://www.gwu.edu/~nsarchiv/coldwar/interviews/episode21/aldrich1.html.

p. 212: a third of the thirty-four anti-virus programs: http://theepochtimes.com/n2/content/view/14459.

p. 212: "relatively simple . . . meticulous": Jeremy Wagstaff, "Digital Espionage — Off the Shelf," *Jakarta Post,* April 20, 2009.

p. 212: "dubs the . . . dragon'": http://www.wired.com/threatlevel/2009/03/spy-system-focu.

p. 212: "a propaganda campaign": "China Denies Spying Allegations," BBC News, March 30, 2009. http://bbc.co.uk/2/hi/americas/7972702.stm.

p. 213: "nonsense": John Markoff, "Vast Spy System Loots Computers in 103 Countries," *New York Times,* March 28, 2009.

p. 216: bold, brave FBI agent in the dark suit": Vise, p. 32.

p. 216: "an oddball out," "very dour," fairly long . . . appearance," and "He was brighter . . . the Bureau": Vise, p. 81.

p. 217: "one of the smartest FBI agents I ever met": Monica Davey, "Secret Passage, *Chicago Tribune Magazine,* April 21, 2002.

p. 218: "Do Not Open . . . Cherkashin": Vise, p. 70.

p. 220: "If you wish . . . I can call": Vise, p. 82.

p. 222: "He forgot that . . . risk he was" and "valuable . . . the CIA": Vise, p. 207.

p. 225: "Dear Friends . . . active service" and "higher do-nothing . . . program": Vise, p. 214.

p. 226: "What took you so long?": Vise. p. 216.

p. 226: "cooperation concerning . . . problematic": Adrian Havill, "Robert Philip Hanssen: The Spy Who Stayed Out in the Cold," TruTV.com. http://www.trutv.com/library/crime/terrorists_spies/spies/hanssen/14.html.

p. 227: "five-hundred-year flood" and "as artful a spy . . . been caught": Vise, pp. 241 and 238.

Bibliography

Allen, Thomas B. *George Washington, Spymaster.* Washington, D.C.: National Geographic, 2004.

Ambrose, Stephen E. *Ike's Spies: Eisenhower and the Espionage Establishment.* Jackson, MS: University of Mississippi Press, 1999.

Andrew, Christopher M. *For the President's Eyes Only.* New York: HarperCollins, 1995.

Axelrod, Alan. *The War between the Spies.* New York: Atlantic Monthly Press, 1992.

Bakeless, John. *Spies of the Confederacy.* Philadelphia: Lippincott, 1970.

———. *Turncoats, Traitors, and Heroes.* Philadelphia: Lippincott, 1960.

Bamford, James. *Body of Secrets.* New York: Doubleday, 2001.

Beesly, Patrick. *Room 40: British Naval Intelligence, 1914–1918.* San Diego: Harcourt Brace Jovanovich, 1982.

Bennett, Richard M. *Espionage: An Encyclopedia of Secrets.* London: Vergin Books, 2008.

Binney, Marcus. *The Women Who Lived for Danger.* New York: William Morrow, 2002.

Blackman, Ann. *Wild Rose: Rose O'Neale Greenhow, Civil War Spy.* New York: Random House, 2005.

Coleman, Janet Wyman. *Secrets, Lies, Gizmos, and Spies.* New York: Abrams, 2006.

Davies, Barry. *The Spycraft Manual.* St. Paul, MN: Zenith Press, 2005.

Dorril, Stephen. *MI6: Inside the Covert World of Her Majesty's Secret Intelligence Service.* New York: Free Press, 2000.

Dulles, Allen W. *The Craft of Intelligence.* Guilford, CT: Lyons Press, 2006.

———, ed. *Great Spy Stories from Fiction.* New York: Harper & Row, 1969.

Feis, William B. *Grant's Secret Service.* Lincoln, NE: University of Nebraska Press, 2002.

Fishel, Edwin C. *The Secret War for the Union.* Boston: Houghton Mifflin, 1996.

Ford, Corey. *A Peculiar Service.* Boston: Little, Brown, 1965.

Haufler, Hervie. *The Spies Who Never Were.* New York: NAL Caliber, 2006.

Hunter, Ryan Ann. *In Disguise! Stories of Real Women Spies.* Hillsboro, OR: Beyond Words Publishing, 2003.

Huntington, Thomas. "The Berlin Spy Tunnel Affair," *Invention & Technology Magazine,* spring 1995. http://www.americanheritage .com/articles/magazine/it/1995/4/1995_4_44.shtml

International Spy Museum. *Spying: The Secret History of History.* New York: Black Dog & Leventhal, 2004.

Kahn, David. *The Codebreakers.* New York: Scribner, 1967.

Keegan, John. *Intelligence in War.* New York: Knopf, 2003.

Knightley, Philip. *The Second Oldest Profession.* New York: Norton, 1987.

Markle, Donald E. *Spies and Spymasters of the Civil War.* New York: Hippocrene Books, 2004.

Masterman, J. C. *The Double-Cross System.* New York: Lyons Press, 2000.

McIntosh, Elizabeth P. *Sisterhood of Spies.* Annapolis, MD: Naval Institute Press, 1998.

Melton, H. Keith. *The Ultimate Spy Book.* New York: DK Publishing, 1996.

Nash, Jay Robert. *Spies.* New York: M. Evans, 1997.

O'Donnell, Patrick K. *Operatives, Spies, and Saboteurs.* New York: Free Press, 2004.

O'Toole, G. J. A. *The Encyclopedia of American Intelligence and Espionage.* New York: Facts on File, 1988.

———. *Honorable Treachery.* New York: Atlantic Monthly Press, 1991.

Owen, David. *Hidden Secrets.* Buffalo, NY: Firefly Books, 2002.

Pedlow, Gregory, and Donald E. Welzenbach. *The CIA and the U-2 Program, 1954–1974.* Washington, D.C.: Central Intelligence Agency, 1998.

Persico, Joseph E. *Piercing the Reich.* New York: Viking, 1979.

Polmar, Norman, and Thomas B. Allen. *Spy Book: The Encyclopedia of Espionage.* New York: Random House, 1997.

Powers, Thomas. *Intelligence Wars.* New York: New York Review Books, 2002.

Prados, John. *Presidents' Secret Wars.* New York: Morrow, 1986.

Proctor, Tammy M. *Female Intelligence: Women and Espionage in the First World War.* New York: New York University Press, 2003.

Pujol, Juan, and Nigel West. *Garbo.* London: Grafton Books, 1986.

Randall, Willard Sterne. *Benedict Arnold: Patriot and Traitor.* New York: Morrow, 1990.

Richelson, Jeffrey T. *A Century of Spies.* New York: Oxford University Press, 1995.

———. *The Wizards of Langley.* Boulder, CO: Westview Press, 2001.

Rose, Alexander. *Washington's Spies.* New York: Bantam, 2006.

Ryan, David D., ed. *A Yankee Spy in Richmond.* Mechanicsburg, PA: Stackpole Books, 1996.

Sayers, Michael, and Albert E. Kahn. *Sabotage! The Secret War Against America.* New York: Harper, 1942.

Senate Select Committee on Intelligence. "An Assessment of the Aldrich H. Ames Espionage Case and Its Implications to U.S. Intelligence," November 1, 1994. http://www.fas.org/irp/congress/1994_rpt/ssci_ames.htm.

Smith, Richard Harris. *OSS: The Secret History of America's First Central Intelligence Agency.* Guilford, CT: Lyons Press, 2005.

Stafford, David. *Spies Beneath Berlin.* Woodstock, NY: Overlook Press, 2003.

Stern, Philip Van Doren. *Secret Missions of the Civil War.* Chicago: Rand McNally, 1959.

Taubman, Philip. *Secret Empire.* New York: Simon & Schuster, 2003.

Tuchman, Barbara W. *The Zimmermann Telegram.* New York: Macmillan, 1958.

Van Doren, Carl. *Secret History of the American Revolution.* New York: Viking, 1941.

Varon, Elizabeth R. *Southern Lady, Yankee Spy.* New York: Oxford University Press, 2003.

Vise, David A. *The Bureau and the Mole.* New York: Atlantic Monthly Press, 2002.

Volkman, Ernest. *Spies.* New York: Wiley, 1994.

Wallace, Robert, and H. Keith Melton. *Spycraft.* New York: Dutton, 2008.

Weiner, Tim. *Legacy of Ashes: The History of the CIA.* New York: Doubleday, 2007.

Wise, David. *Nightmover.* New York: HarperCollins, 1995.

Witcover, Jules. *Sabotage at Black Tom.* Chapel Hill, NC: Algonquin Books, 1989.

Wright, Peter. *Spycatcher.* New York: Viking, 1987.

Photography Credits

Index

Cassava bread and bush tea mixed with milk. The mistress. Six months, six weeks, six days, it mattered little for her status was secure. The mistress, she had a position, but they would never learn to read and understand her strange moods. And now fallen upon curious times, standing alone and listening to the voices that disturbed the night. Papa, was he dead? His endless pleas for her to return. To Thomas Lockwood? Papa dead? No. Would she be forgiven for her indiscretion? There was once a threat of impending arrival transported to her by a sad Mr Wilson. He could not lift his eyes to meet the glare in hers. Doomed. She laughed at him. He looked as though he might shed tears. And then Mr Wilson rode off and never came again to visit. And Papa's threat was never executed. And now? Was the pleading at an end? I'm still here. Emily gestured, palms upturned, eyebrows arched. Are there no ships that might take me away? But take me away to what and to whom? She giggled. A man strung up, mouth agape, tongue protruding. Hercules. Cambridge. With his Bible. Murderer. A slow chill rippled through her body. ('Please keep still and stop talking. Stop talking.') To encourage the delicate head of a child to lie peacefully in the shallow valley between her fallen breasts. But not now. The head ballooning out of her body into the earth. Emily squashed a mosquito against her arm, brushed it to the floor, and wiped away the blood with the back of her hand. Her autumnal eccentricities. Premature. Turning the last corner of beauty. Stella claimed that the estate would be sold off in small plots to free whites and mulattoes (and negroes who could afford such things). Ah, thought Emily. Ship? Useless thoughts fell quietly like over-ripe fruit into freshly lain snow. Snow-white face, unseen snow, never again. Emily. Miss Emily. Emily Cartwright. Emily. Emily. Inside of me once. The little foreigner now no longer resident in my womb. I speak and Isabella answers, and now silence. Emily listened. In this small cottage she listened carefully but heard nothing above the noises of the night. Quick, come quick, death. Emily understood that the patient ones decentre quietly and with more beauty. I have been patient. Quick, come quick. Quick.

Emily stood before the mirror. And now sunrise. She knew that she must bear the weight of yet another day. She knew that she must endure the undignified mêlée of dawn. She knew that, in all likelihood, she would have to witness the dying of the sun come dusk. She understood this. The fragrance of poinsettia came wafting into the room in small eddies that caused the light in the lamp to dance in tune to the scent. She remembered. Journeying up the hill to Hawthorn Cottage. With her friend. Stella. Dear Stella.